Working with Young Homeless People

of related interest

Residential Child Care
Prospects and Challenges
Edited by Andrew Kendrick
ISBN 978 1 84310 526 8
Research Highlights in Social Work 47

Server User Involvement
Reaching the Hard to Reach in Supported Housing
Helen Brafield and Terry Eckersley
ISBN 978 1 84310 343 1

Mental Health Interventions and Services for Vulnerable Children
and Young People
Edited by Panos Vostanis
ISBN 978 1 84310 489 6

Working with Anger and Young People
Nick Luxmoore
ISBN 978 1 84310 466 7

Leaving Care
Throughcare and Aftercare in Scotland
Jo Dixon and Mike Stein
ISBN 978 1 84310 202 1

Young People's Transitions from Care to Adulthood
International Research and Practice
Edited by Mike Stein and Emily R. Munro
ISBN 978 1 84310 610 4
Child Welfare Outcomes series

Homeless Children
Problems and Needs
Edited by Panos Vostanis and Stuart Cumella
ISBN 978 1 85302 595 2

'Race', Housing and Social Exclusion
Edited by Peter Somerville and Andy Steele
ISBN 978 1 85302 849 6

Working with Young Homeless People

Phil Robinson

Jessica Kingsley Publishers
London and Philadelphia

First published in 2008
by Jessica Kingsley Publishers
116 Pentonville Road
London N1 9JB, UK
and
400 Market Street, Suite 400
Philadelphia, PA 19106, USA

www.jkp.com

Library of Congress Cataloging in Publication Data
A CIP catalog record for this book is available from the Library of Congress

British Library Cataloguing in Publication Data
A CIP catalogue record for this book is available from the British Library

ISBN 978 1 84310 611 1

Printed and bound in Great Britain by
Athenaeum Press, Gateshead, Tyne and Wear

Contents

Acknowledgements

This book was developed from a thesis which I submitted to Strathclyde University for my PhD. Its primary subject matter was a peer research project carried out in Glasgow over a period of 18 months. A good deal of the material collected by that project is included in this book, so I would like to thank all of the young people who became involved in that project in various ways, but especially the peer researchers who, in a very real sense, made it 'their project'. Without their contribution, this book would certainly not have been written. I would also like to thank Professor Andy Kendrick for his wise guidance and unfailing support, Avril Mudie, a very keen and committed research assistant, and my employer, Quarriers, for their generous sponsorship.

The help of my colleagues in Quarriers Youth Housing Practice Development Group, who read and commented with real insight into various chapters, has been invaluable, as has that of Louisa McSherry in the preparation of the final manuscript.

Finally I must thank my wife Nancy, daughter Gail and sons Thomas and Ewan for help in so many ways, not least putting up with this obsession over so many years.

Introduction

What is this Book About?

Young people who become homeless seem to enter a world that is little known to outsiders and from which it is difficult to escape. They seem to occupy a sort of 'limbo' state in which they remain whilst being helped to prepare for fully independent living. It was my curiosity about the nature of this twilight world and the effect it has upon its inhabitants – nurtured by the experience of undertaking an earlier research study on care leavers and homelessness and many years spent developing and managing services for young homeless people – which prompted me to begin a research study that ultimately led to this book for practitioners.

Many young homeless people are known to experience great difficulty in their attempts to break free, often progressing to the stage of taking on their own tenancy, only to lose it and begin again the cycle of hostels and supported accommodation. Even quite sophisticated professional support services seem powerless to intervene in this process and this may be because the elements that are missing from young people's lives are the ones that no professional has the power to provide.

This book is a practical guide and resource for those working in services for young homeless people. It utilises the views and insights of young homeless people – gathered through a small-scale research project sponsored by Quarriers, the Scottish social care charity (see Appendix – woven together with a distillation of my own experience and that of many of my colleagues in these services. The book should also provide a useful resource for students from a variety of academic and vocational disciplines who wish to learn more about the largely hidden world of youth homelessness and what can be done about it.

1

What is Youth Homelessness?

There is no universally accepted definition of homelessness and this naturally makes life very difficult for all who have an in-depth concern about the issue. For example, one of the main constraints in developing reliable estimates of the extent of homelessness is this variation in the way that homelessness is defined. Should the term be limited to those who are 'living on the street', as many members of the general public might argue, or does the term 'homeless' encompass many more hidden (and numerous) groups of individuals, who do not have a settled home?

The element of dissociation in the use of the term 'the homeless', rather than 'homeless people' or 'people without homes', discloses a dehumanising process. By this means we – members of this society – are able to distance ourselves from the emotional responses provoked by contact with people who are seen as failing to conform to social norms and having offended public sensibilities.

Daly (1996) expresses the view that a 'liberal' definition would be: 'People are considered homeless if they lack adequate shelter in which they are entitled to live safely' (Daly 1996, p.1). Daly also argues, persuasively, that definitions of homelessness expose prevailing values and beliefs rather than provide clarity about the phenomenon itself, and this will not make our task any easier. In this chapter, therefore, we can only hope to provide some clarity about the ways in which differing definitions have been used and the impact these have had upon the issue itself.

We shall also consider the clandestine nature of the phenomenon and difficulties this poses in trying to measure its extent.

Who are the homeless?

All of the following terms, and the scenarios that they describe, can be considered definitions of homelessness (Fitzpatrick, Kemp and Klinker 2000):

- 'Rooflessness', or the lack of any shelter of any kind. This definition includes people who are sleeping rough and is the narrowest definition of homelessness.

- 'Houselessness', a term which includes people who are living in all forms of emergency or institutional accommodation, solely because they do not have access to mainstream housing.

- Lack of secure tenure, including those staying temporarily with friends or relatives and squatters.

- Intolerable housing conditions, such as overcrowded and substandard accommodation, as well as situations involving threats to an individual's safety or wellbeing.

- Sharing of accommodation on a long-term basis, not through choice, but because of the inability to access separate housing.

Taken together, these five terms form a very broad definition of homelessness, covering most aspects of housing need, but this definition does not necessarily coincide with the way in which the term 'homelessness' is generally or even frequently used. In fact, most members of the general public would probably use a narrower definition and many would not stray far from the first term in the list, 'rooflessness'. All of these terms fail to address the emotional and social dimensions of homelessness, however. In subsequent chapters we shall find that an individual's definition of him- or herself as a homeless person may have a profound impact upon many aspects of his or her life and also that groups of people brought together by a common experience of homelessness may have distinct and pervasive social characteristics.

Some commentators have highlighted the danger that referring to all housing need as homelessness masks the essential difference between the experience of having inadequate housing and that of having no housing at all (Pleace 1997). Whilst the secure tenure of a safe and comfortable home is a basic human need and the impact of the lack of it can hardly be overestimated, there are clearly deeper levels of trauma and dehumanisation associated with the various manifestations of homelessness. The most extreme of these are associated with 'rooflessness' – the state of living 'on the street' – although, as we shall see (below), this accounts for a comparatively small proportion of young homeless people.

Without agreement about what constitutes a 'home', there can be no agreed definition of homelessness since, at its simplest, 'homelessness' means 'not having a home'. This is a highly subjective issue and, although factors such as safety and security constantly reoccur, everyone's definition of 'home' tends to differ from everyone else's.

Excluded categories

Due to the transitory, unstable lifestyle that is forced upon homeless people, they can be difficult to contact and therefore difficult to quantify. Definitions that are sometimes used to facilitate counting at a crude level can mean that some categories of homeless people are excluded from active concern and consideration – for example, using the statistics of agencies working with the homeless as a measure of homelessness. Such statistics can only be regarded as accurate if one assumes that every young homeless person is in touch with one or more of the agencies tasked with providing services for them. Hutson and Liddiard (1994) argue that this practice excludes young women and young black people who often use strategies to deal with their homelessness that do not include contact with these agencies:

> The key to understanding the relative invisibility of young women and young black people in such homelessness statistics is to understand more about the nature of their homelessness. For example, women tend to use hostels less than men. In the first place, there may be fewer beds available for them and, if there is provision, women may not feel safe in such accommodation. Similarly, young people from ethnic minority groups are often unwilling to use hostels which may be in white areas, with predominantly white staff. (Hutson and Liddiard 1994, p.43)

Hence these groups of homeless people may be significantly under-represented in official statistics and this goes some way towards explaining why attaining a comprehensive picture of youth homelessness is so difficult.

Young women and young black people are often included in the commonly used term, 'the hidden homeless'. Other 'hidden homeless' include those who have not applied for public housing and those who sleep rough, away from visible areas and known sites. These categories of homeless people contribute to the great difficulty in quantifying homelessness, but Fitzpatrick *et al.* (2000) argue that the definition of their homelessness may fall within quite narrow parameters. It is not, therefore, that inclusion of the hidden homeless implies a broad definition, but rather that homeless people are simply almost impossible to count.

What do homeless people themselves say?

Only a few studies have addressed the way homeless people define themselves and these studies appear to disagree on the subject. Hutson and Liddiard (1994) found that young homeless people often interpreted homelessness narrowly as rough sleeping and it was common for those staying with friends not to describe themselves as homeless. Fitzpatrick (2000), on the other hand, reported that young people involved in her study generally adopted a broader definition of homelessness as having 'no permanent house' and added to this with their own concepts of 'home'. She quotes one of the young people involved in her study as follows: 'Knowing the people around you, like your neighbours, and knowing the area. Like I wouldnae like tae be in an area I didnae know anybody...don't think I could call that a home' (Fitzpatrick 2000, p.36). Fitzpatrick goes on to contend that: 'The main components of these young people's definitions of home can be summarised as follows: a safe and/or familiar neighbourhood; security and permanence of tenancy; independence, control and privacy; decent material conditions; homeliness and personalization; and family' (Fitzpatrick 2000, p.37).

This is a fairly all-encompassing list and underlines the fact that there can be no complete understanding of homeless people's own conceptions of homelessness since, like any of us, they will always prioritise different aspects of the multifaceted concept that is 'home'. Most studies do agree, however, that 'security' and 'permanence' are factors that are emphasised more often than the physical conditions of a dwelling or potential dwelling. It comes as no surprise that in the final analysis a 'safe home' beats a 'nice home', hands down, every time.

Measuring the scale of the problem

There is no national census of homeless people in Britain and the published statistics on homelessness tend to fluctuate quite markedly, but it should be remembered that the figure for the number of people recorded as homeless is often defined as: '[The] total number of individuals accessing services who were homeless at the point of contact' (Glasgow Homelessness Network 2002/2003, p.7).

In other words, those who may lack a permanent, secure home, but have not come to the attention of the relevant agencies dealing with the homeless, are excluded. The initial focus of attention tended to be on rough sleepers and therefore produced only a partial indicator of the numbers of people homeless, but the subsequent broader definition still did not provide an accurate and universally agreed assessment of numbers. To date, no such widely accepted means of conceptualising and measuring homelessness has been achieved, either for the UK as a whole, or for Scotland (Pleace 1997).

The only national data source is the information returned quarterly by local authorities to the UK Department of the Environment (DOE), which subsequently became the Office of the Deputy Prime Minister (ODPM), although a further change means that homelessness is now the responsibility of the UK Department for Communities and Local Government (DCLG). The statistics show that in the years between 1971, when their collection commenced, and 1986 the number of applications to local authorities in England and Wales for housing by homeless households increased from 33,386 to 220,240 (Drake 1989). A number of caveats must be borne in mind when considering these data, however. For part of the period, local authorities were required only to help those defined as 'in priority need' by the Housing (Homeless Persons) Act 1977. Vulnerability was not defined by the Act in such a way as to include all of those who may actually have been vulnerable and homeless. Young people, for example, were not considered vulnerable on the basis of their age alone and do not feature as a category of homeless people in the DOE statistics. For this reason, these statistics are likely to provide a serious underestimate of the actual number of people homeless.

Legislative definitions of homelessness

National policies on homelessness, as set out in key pieces of legislation such as the Housing Act 1996 in the UK, or the McKinney Act in the USA, frequently contain definitions of homelessness, as well as a delineation of the responsibilities that the state accepts towards the homeless (Hutson and Liddiard 1994). Where there is a statutory responsibility, statistics are likely to be collected and surveys and accounts of homelessness will focus on those categories of people for whom the government has responsibility. In the USA, for example, numbers and accounts are predominantly of shelter users, often older single men, whereas in the UK the focus is primarily on homeless families. In both countries, young single people have very largely been omitted.

In England and Wales, the Housing Act 1996 governs housing allocations and duties towards those who are homeless. The definition of homelessness is still governed by Part 7 of this Act. A person is considered homeless if he or she, together with any person he or she lives with, has no accommodation which he or she is entitled to occupy and which it would be reasonable for he or she to continue to occupy. Those likely to become homeless within 28 days qualify under the Act, as well as those already homeless, and the basic duty placed upon local authorities is to provide advice, assistance and, in certain circumstances, accommodation for the homeless. The Act places a statutory obligation upon local authorities to provide suitable accommodation for any person who meets its four criteria. The person must be eligible for assistance, homeless, in priority need of accommodation, and not intentionally homeless.

Where the housing authority believes that the applicant meets the first three of these criteria it has an interim duty to provide accommodation while enquiries are ongoing. If satisfied that the applicant is eligible for assistance but became homeless intentionally, they must provide advice and assistance to help the applicant find accommodation. In England, Wales and Scotland the principle of intentionality absolves the local authority from the duty to accommodate. Some amendments in the ways in which local authorities are required to exercise their responsibilities towards the homeless were introduced by the Homelessness Act 2002 but the most important change, for our present purposes, was effected by the Homelessness (Priority Need for Accommodation) (England) Order 2002. Six more criteria of priority need were introduced under this Order and the following are now considered to be 'in priority need':

1. A pregnant woman or someone with whom she resides or may reasonably be expected to reside.

2. A person with whom dependent children reside or may be expected to reside (including a child who could be reasonably expected to if the applicant had a home).

3. A person who is vulnerable as a result of old age, mental illness or handicap, or physical disability, or who has some other special reason for being vulnerable or with whom such a person resides or may reasonably be expected to reside.

4. A person whose homelessness, or threatened homelessness, results from flood, fire or similar emergency or disaster.

5. A person aged 16 or 17 who is not a relevant child or a child in need to whom the local authority owes a duty under s.20 of the Children Act 1989.

6. A person under 21 who was (but is no longer) looked after, accommodated or fostered between the ages of 16 and 18 (except a person who is a 'relevant student').

7. A person aged 21 or more who is vulnerable as a result of having been looked after.

8. A person who is vulnerable as a result of having been a member of Her Majesty's regular naval, military or air forces.

9. A person who is vulnerable as a result of: (i) having served a custodial sentence; (ii) having been committed for contempt of court or any other kindred offence; (iii) having been remanded in custody.

10. A person who is vulnerable as a result of ceasing to occupy accommodation because of violence or threats of violence from another person which are likely to be carried out.

For the first time, these criteria included the principle that some young people should be considered as being in priority need purely because of their extreme youth (see '5', above).

In Wales, a slightly different set of definitions applies, under the Homeless Persons (Priority Need) (Wales) Order, introduced by the National Assembly for Wales in 2001, but they are substantially the same in relation to young people.

In Scotland, the Housing (Scotland) Act 1987 dealt comprehensively with homelessness in Part 2 which included a list of groups of people who should be regarded as being vulnerable for special reasons and hence in priority need (Section 25(1) para 7.3). The list was also included in the Codes of Guidance published in 1991 and 1997 (Scottish Office 1991, 1997) and was broadly similar to that applying under English legislation but did not include young people. Once again, youth was clearly not, in itself, regarded as sufficient cause for an individual to be considered vulnerable and in priority need of housing.

This situation did not change with the next piece of legislation in Scotland addressing issues relevant to homelessness – The Housing (Scotland) Act 2003 – but this was soon followed by the Homelessness etc (Scotland) Act 2003. Only then was the list of priority need categories expanded to include: 'All those who are under 18 or who have been subject to harassment or domestic abuse, people under 21 who are vulnerable to financial or sexual exploitation or involvement in substance misuse due to their living circumstances' (Scottish Executive 2003).

This section of the Act came into force on 30 January 2004 and the consequent revised Code of Guidance (Scottish Executive 2005) was only published in May 2005, so it is too early to assess the impact of this legislation. It seems incredible, however, that from the time that youth homelessness emerged as a significant social issue, over 25 years elapsed before young people were recognised as vulnerable in legislation designed to address the problem of homelessness.

Finally, building on the framework created by this legislation in Scotland, Malcolm Chisholm's ministerial statement in December 2005 (Scottish Executive 2005) announced the planned reduction of the proportion of non-priority assessments by 50 per cent by 2009 and the eradication of the distinction between 'priority' and 'non-priority' homeless households by the end of 2012. This will mean that all unintentionally homeless people will be entitled to permanent accommodation at that time. At the time of writing, no similar move has been made by the Westminster Government to abolish the concept of priority need in England, nor by the Welsh Assembly in Wales.

The influence of policy on statistics

It can be seen from the foregoing that policy towards homeless people has changed significantly over the last 30 years and that official statistics reflect a policy-determined reality to some extent. Furthermore, many of the local authorities with the heaviest burdens of homelessness did not send the relevant statistical returns to the DOE and the numbers for these authorities had to be estimated (Drake 1989). Despite these caveats, it is clear that the numbers of homeless people within our society did increase rapidly during the years in question and that much of the increase was accounted for by rising numbers of single homeless people. The percentage of single people within the total number of households accepted as homeless increased from 13 per cent in 1975 to 45 per cent in 1986 (DOE Homelessness Statistics, cited by Drake 1989) but, as explained above, this category did not include young people and was largely made up of the elderly and the ill.

The focus eventually broadened from rough sleepers to other less obvious groups of young homeless people, including those who were staying 'care of' other householders and were therefore not included in the homelessness statistics. As early as 1989, a study found that this category especially applied to women and could account for as many as 3000 single women under the age of 26 on Glasgow District Council's waiting list (Scottish Council for the Single Homeless 1989). This was a most important finding, as was a further finding contained within the same report that showed, by following up a sample of applicants from selected districts, that few received any offer of housing and those who did were usually offered housing in the 'hard to let' category. Saxton and Evans (2002) suggest that homeless acceptances by local authorities appeared to have hit a peak in 1991 and then declined. While homelessness acceptances have not reached these levels again (though they are now rising again, from a low in 1997), the increased use of temporary accommodation as a percentage of all acceptances in this period is striking. It only accounted for 8 per cent of all acceptances in 1981, but 45 per cent in 1991 and nearly 75 per cent in 2000. A report from Crisis (Crisis Campaigns 2001, cited by Saxton and Evans 2002) suggests that there might be a total of around 400,000 hidden homeless. The Crisis figures are from a variety of sources, some of which are included in the figures from local authorities and some of which are not. They highlight a number of areas where the official figures from local authorities fail to take account of, and demonstrate just how difficult it is to reliably estimate, the extent of homelessness within any defined area.

Young runaways

A separate but closely related strand of research concerns 'young runaways', defined as: 'Young people under 17 years, or in local authority care under 19 years, who leave home or residential care of their own accord but without agreement, or are forced to leave home, and are missing for one or more nights' (Newman 1988, p.1). This very specific definition highlighted the needs of an exceptionally vulnerable subgroup, many of whom are also likely to be included within definitions of the young homeless. Many parallels and crossovers are evident when these accounts of young runaways are read alongside studies of young homeless people, including the author's recent research (Robinson 2006). The reasons young runaways give for running away are broadly similar to those given by young homeless people for leaving home, with both groups emphasising factors such as domestic conflict, violence and abuse (Newman 1988). Few young people become homeless without experiencing one or more of these issues. Furthermore, young runaways frequently come to the attention of agencies dealing with young homeless people and are recorded as such.

The two categories may diverge around the length of time that a young person has been or is likely to be in the situation being defined. The definition of young runaways (above) includes those who have been away from home for only one night and for whom there is no insuperable barrier to their return home. Young homeless people are usually regarded as being in a more prolonged situation, because they do not have a viable home to return to, or because the nature of their home may make return dangerous or unpalatable.

Ultimately the term 'young runaway' is an unhelpful one that has more to do with the generation of funding for voluntary sector projects than with identifying a distinctive subgroup. There are dangers inherent in the use of this term, however, in that those unfamiliar with the overlaps between those termed 'young homeless' and those termed 'young runaways' might well regard the latter as a group in greater need of support than the former.

Learning points

- There is no single, agreed, definition of homelessness.

- Many more people lack a settled home than those forced to sleep rough, but the definitions used often expose values prevailing within society.

- Some categories of 'hidden homelessness' are often excluded from official statistics because they are impossible to quantify.

- Definitions of 'home' also vary widely but most homeless people emphasise safety, security and familiarity above material conditions.

- There is no national census of homeless people in the UK and few reliable statistics.

- Published data tend to rely on numbers of those known to use services for the homeless, hence excluding many others.

- Governments tend to collect statistics primarily on those for whom they have a statutory responsibility. This has changed over time as awareness and legislation have developed.

- The term 'young runaways' has been the focus of some specific research but many young runaways are young homeless people and vice versa.

- The development of the phenomenon of youth homelessness in other economically developed countries has been broadly similar to that in the UK.

- International comparisons are virtually impossible due to variations in definitions and data collection.

Conclusion

As there is no universally accepted definition as to what constitutes a homeless young person, there can be no comprehensive and accurate measure of the scale of the problem. During the early years of the youth homelessness crisis, in the late 1980s and early 1990s, however, a number of attempts were made to generate some hard data, through surveys of various kinds. These were extremely useful, however incomplete and flawed they may have been. Commentators continue to return to survey data over ten years old in order to try to understand the many facets of the issue. It seems strange that survey activity seems to have virtually dried up in the intervening period, and it may be that this is partly due to the near impossibility of the task. The reduction in the number of young people visibly rough-sleeping on the streets of British cities may have removed the incentive to carry out expensive, quantitative research on a large scale.

References

Daly, G. (1996) *Homeless: Policies, Strategies and Lives on the Street*. London: Routledge.

Drake, M. (1989) 'Fifteen years of homelessness in the UK.' *Housing Studies 4*, 2, 119–127.

Fitzpatrick, S. (2000) *Young Homeless People*. Basingstoke: Macmillan.

Fitzpatrick, S., Kemp, P. and Klinker, S. (2000) *Single Homelessness: An Overview of Research in Britain*. Bristol: Policy Press.

Glasgow Homelessness Network (2002) *National Rough Sleeping Initiative Core Data Report, 01 April 2002–30 September 2002*. Glasgow: Glasgow Homelessness Network.

Glasgow Homelessness Network (2003) *National Rough Sleeping Initiative Core Data Report, 01 April 2003–30 September 2003*. Glasgow: Glasgow Homelessness Network.

Hutson, S. and Liddiard, M. (1994) *Youth Homelessness: The Construction of a Social Reality*. Basingstoke: Macmillan.

Newman, C. (1988) *Young Runaways: Findings from Britain's First Safe House*. London: Children's Society.

Pleace, N. (1997) 'Homelessness in contemporary Britain: Conceptualisation and measurement.' In R. Burrows, N. Pleace and D. Quilgars (eds) *Homelessness and Social Policy*. London: Routledge.

Robinson, P.H. (2006) 'Young homeless people: The importance of informal support networks in their daily lives.' Unpublished PhD thesis.

Saxton, J. and Evans, E. (2002) *The Future of Homelessness? The External Environment and its Impact on Homelessness*. Briefing paper on the future of homelessness as part of the London Housing Foundation's IMPACT programme. London: nfpSynergy.

Scottish Council for the Single Homeless (1989) *Women's Homelessness – The Hidden Problem*. Edinburgh: SCSH.

Scottish Executive (2003) *The Homelessness etc (Scotland) Act (2003)*. London: HMSO.

Scottish Executive (2005) *Helping Homeless People*. Homelessness Statement. Ministerial statement on abolition of priority need by 2012. Edinburgh: Scottish Executive.

Scottish Office (1991/1997) *Homelessness: Code of Guidance for Local Authorities*. Edinburgh: Scottish Office.

2

The Characteristics of Young Homeless People

Many assumptions are made about young people who are homeless. For example, it is often thought that they are likely to be involved in alcohol and drug abuse, or more likely to be involved than other young people of similar age group in the general population (see Chapter 8). It is very important in a book such as this to separate the truth from the myth and, as far as possible, set out the facts.

The most recent major survey of homelessness in the UK was conducted as long ago as 1991 (Anderson, Kemp and Quilgars 1993). This study focused on ten local authority areas in England and attempted to make comparisons between several distinct groups of single homeless people, including people living in hostels and bed and breakfast accommodation and rough sleepers. The study did not include any specific focus on young homeless people, however, and had a strong accommodation focus, with only limited attention given to wider support needs. Before the 1991 survey, one must go back to 1981 to find the next most recent large-scale, rigorous survey of single homeless people in England and, in many respects, little had changed since then. The majority of people sleeping rough were still found to be white, middle-aged and male. Despite the paucity of accurate, up-to-date information we shall, in this chapter, try to gather together evidence from a wide variety of sources about the characteristics of young people who find themselves in this unfortunate position.

Age group

In a survey of two large hostels for the homeless in London in 1970, 22 per cent of a sample of 123 residents was found to be over 60 years of age, whilst the mean age of the sample was 46.7 years (Lodge Patch 1971). The 1991 survey (Anderson *et al.* 1993) showed that the proportion of young people, amongst the homeless, was increasing, with people under 25 heavily represented amongst those resident in hostels and bed and breakfast establishments. Smaller numbers of young people were found amongst samples of rough sleepers. These data suggest, therefore, that 16- and 17-year-olds were significantly less likely to be homeless than the slightly older group and that homeless young people generally were less likely to sleep rough for any extended period of time than older homeless people.

Although no large-scale survey has attempted to quantify the overall numbers of homeless people in the UK since 1991, the voluntary sector continued to collect data throughout the 1990s. Their findings have generally confirmed those of Anderson *et al.* (1993) and have indicated that the number of young people, and particularly young women, among the single homeless continued to increase throughout the decade. An evaluation of night shelters, called 'Open Houses', that had been established by the charity Crisis (Pleace and Quilgars 1999) was conducted on a much smaller scale than the 1991 survey but did provide data on 404 young people who used five night shelters. It seemed to suggest a further increase in the proportion of young people and young women amongst the homeless: 29 per cent of all residents were under 25 years of age and 6 per cent were under 18.

The Rough Sleepers Initiative collected data from provider organisations, but its final evaluation (see also Chapter 4) is somewhat critical of the monitoring process that it employed:

> The GHN monitoring lacks sufficient outcome measures, it collects insufficient information from an insufficient number of organisations. Both the range of data collection and the response rate need to be improved. (Fitzpatrick, Pleace and Bevan 2005, p.12)

Nevertheless, the statistical information on homelessness collected by the Rough Sleepers Initiative in Glasgow is interesting, in that it shows that whilst most categories of homelessness were in decline, including an overall reduction of 15 per cent in rough sleeping, over the two years 2000/01 and 2001/02, the under-20 and 60 to 69 age groups were the only ones that showed an increase. In September 2003, a total of 2868 homeless people were recorded in the cumulative statistics from many, but not all, districts of Scotland. Of these, 625 individuals were under the age of 20, whilst 1362 were recorded as rough sleepers (Glasgow Homelessness Network 2003). These figures are subject to seasonal and other fluctuations but, in terms of trends, the returns for the equivalent six-month period ending in September 2002 show that overall figures had increased from 2419 homeless and the number for rough sleepers from 1306, whilst the number of homeless people under 20 had risen from 503 (Glasgow Homelessness Network 2002).

To summarise, there has been a gradual increase in the number of young people recorded amongst those admitted to hostels and bed and breakfast establishments as homeless persons. From a baseline of no young people being recorded in the early 1970s, the proportion of people under 25 had risen to 31 per cent by 1991. The increase in young people sleeping rough was much less marked, but there is some evidence of a significant increase, during the 1990s, mainly affecting the 18 to 25 age group. Since 2000 the available data suggest that every category of homelessness is decreasing, except for young people under 20, in relation to whom the numbers recorded as homeless continue to increase.

Ethnic origin

The 1991 survey (Anderson *et al.* 1993) found that young people who were homeless were much more likely than the general population to be from a black and minority ethnic (BME) background. These findings were to some extent influenced by the survey's urban, and particularly London, focus since people from BME backgrounds form a larger proportion of the population in London and major cities than in small towns and rural areas. This finding was, however, the result of single homelessness also appearing to be concentrated in these same metropolitan and urban areas. The survey showed that 40 per cent of single homeless people living in hostels and B&Bs at that time were from a

BME background, compared with 5 per cent of the general population. Kemp (1997) comments that, by comparing the results of the 1991 survey with the 1972 survey of hostels and common lodging houses (Department of Health and Social Security 1972), a major increase in the proportion of homelessness accounted for by BME people is evident.

More recent findings seem to confirm this trend, with 57 per cent of young people assisted by the charity Centrepoint being from BME origin, while BME people make up 7 per cent of the population in England. Research into BME homelessness in Scotland found that breakdown in existing relationships seemed to be a common contributory factor. This included deterioration in relationships between older and younger members of extended families and was sometimes exacerbated by overcrowding (Shelter 2005). BME households are estimated to be six times more likely to live in overcrowded conditions than white households. It has also been established that overcrowding is one of the risk factors that can lead to young people becoming homeless. Young people who have to share a room by the age of 12 are three times more likely to become homeless.

Young BME people who are homeless tend to be less visible than young white people because they are less likely to be 'on the street' and sleeping rough and more likely to be staying with friends and relatives (Office of the Deputy Prime Minister [ODPM] 2003).

Gender

Although most research on homelessness has traditionally concentrated on men, a number of studies since the mid-1980s have focused on women (Dibblin 1991; Watson and Austerberry 1986). There has, however, been little research that directly compares the experiences of homeless men with those of homeless women and which could therefore offer a rigorous analysis of gender issues within homelessness. Hence, the traditional view that the higher 'visibility' of single men, compared with single women, amongst the homeless is explained by the more hidden nature of female homelessness cannot be fully substantiated. Although Greve (1991), amongst others, has asserted that women are more likely to conceal their homelessness by staying with friends and relatives, the lack of directly comparable research leaves some uncertainty as to whether males are any less likely to experience this situation. The research conducted by Fitzpatrick (2000), in one of Glasgow's peripheral housing schemes, suggests a radically different conclusion:

> The tentative conclusion is therefore that young women are more willing than young men to approach formal agencies when they find themselves homeless, and thus are less likely to take hidden routes through homelessness than their male counterparts. These conclusions clearly run counter to previous literature which has argued that women, including young women, are more likely than men to deal with their homelessness in hidden ways. (Fitzpatrick 2000, p.78)

A number of studies (Fitzpatrick 2000; Smith *et al.* 1996) have found that, in general, fewer homeless young women sleep rough than homeless young men. Evidence on the wider question of whether young women are more or less likely than young men to become homeless must, however, remain inconclusive.

Economic status and aspirations

Whilst family homelessness is particularly associated with housing market pressures in areas of economic growth, homelessness among young single people is often particularly high in areas of economic decline and high unemployment (Greve 1991). There is some evidence of this in Glasgow, where single males are significantly over-repre-sented in the homeless population compared with the rest of Scotland (Fitzpatrick, Kemp and Clinker 2000). It can, quite reasonably, be deduced that as single males are normally the most economically active group within the population, there is likely to be a connection between their high levels of homelessness and the problems of unemployment within the City, caused by long-term economic decline.

Few young people are able to access full-time employment on leaving school. A study in 1996 found that only 8 per cent of young people entered full-time employment on leaving school at 16 (Allard 1996). Many young homeless people have their employment prospects adversely affected to an even greater extent by a history of insecure accommodation. They are likely to lack information on job availability, as well as experience discrimination from employers. For those living in hostels, the high level of rent paid by Housing Benefit acts as a major disincentive to finding work. Because Housing Benefit tapers off as income rises, every additional pound earned through work yields as little as ten pence in real income. Effectively this means that moving off benefits can actually increase the risk of poverty and debt.

The promotion of 'active citizenship' for the young, including activities such as volunteering, in place of vocational training and employment has also distracted society from the task of ensuring that the young will be skilled-up and in a position to meet future labour market requirements. The overall effect of these changes has been to make it much more likely that those young people who lacked the level of family support envisaged as ideal would meet with serious difficulties, including homelessness.

The 1991 survey (Anderson *et al.* 1993) found that young people living in hostels and B&Bs were almost all economically inactive, with only 12 per cent of respondents in work during the week preceding their interview (Pleace and Quilgars 1999). Despite coping with the problems of homelessness, however, only 16 per cent were not currently looking for work. Reliance on benefits was correspondingly high, with 44 per cent of young people aged 16 or 17, and 60 per cent of those aged 18 to 24, having received Income Support in the last week. Approximately two-thirds of the young people interviewed were receiving Housing Benefit. Issues of economic status and policy, including young people's limited and uneven eligibility for benefits, are almost impossible to separate in interpreting these statistics but, nevertheless, it is clear that very few homeless young people have jobs. Begging was not usually mentioned as a source of income, except by some young people who were in the samples of people sleeping rough.

Saxton and Evans (2002) reviewed a range of indicators for homelessness relating to the UK economy, noting that most were positive. Their overall conclusion is that: 'If the root of homelessness is economic deprivation, the overall outlook for a reduction should be good. If the root of homelessness is more closely linked to a number of other factors such as the housing market, support from social services and level of juvenile crime, the outlook is less positive' (Saxton and Evans 2002, p.18).

Educational background

It is widely recognised that homeless young people find it difficult to access further education. Although few data are available, the possibility clearly arises that this difficulty may limit their employment prospects and contribute to the wider scenario of disadvantage that they face (Velasco 2002). This is not to imply that homeless young people are innately lacking the abilities required to enable them to benefit from educational opportunities but rather that their social and family situation presents a range of barriers. For those moving from one temporary home to another, or sleeping rough, it is almost impossible to sustain training or education programmes because their time is spent finding somewhere to sleep.

Educational disadvantage and school failure have also been found to be factors common to young people who eventually become homeless. Writing about the young people involved in her study of homeless young people in one of the peripheral housing estates in Glasgow, Fitzpatrick (2000) states:

> Almost all the young homeless people I interviewed left school as soon as they could at the end of the fourth year, and many gained no qualifications at all. Truancy was almost universal amongst these young people, particularly at secondary school, but this varied from those who just missed the occasional day to some who hardly ever attended school at all. (Fitzpatrick 2000, p.101)

Others have found that few looked after young people – an important parallel group to young homeless people, in terms of disadvantage, with many crossovers – make it to university. There are no published figures, but the best estimate is fewer than one in one hundred, compared with 37 per cent of those who grow up in their own families (Jackson, Ajayi and Quigley 2003). This is hardly surprising, however, since educational failure is part of the same pattern of disadvantage amongst young people that also includes homelessness and unemployment.

Care background

Surveys have routinely found that between one-fifth and one-half of young homeless people have been in care. Since only 1 per cent of all children and young people have been in care, it is clear that care leavers are much more likely to become homeless than other young people (Clapham and Evans 2000). Hutson and Liddiard (1994) comment that:

> If it is generally accepted that there is a link between leaving home early and homelessness, there is no doubt at all about the close

connection between leaving state child care and homelessness. This link is common to all western industrial countries. (Hutson and Liddiard 1994, p.60)

The actual percentages vary, however. For example, studies by Centrepoint Soho showed that in 1987 23 per cent of young people referring themselves to the night shelter had lived in children's homes (Randall 1988), but in a repeat survey in 1989 the figure had risen to 41 per cent, but with a smaller sample (Randall 1989). Estimates of the proportion of care leavers amongst the ranks of the homeless vary widely because there is no universally agreed definition of what constitutes a 'care leaver'. So, for example, the figure for those who may have experienced public care at some point during their childhood will inevitably be higher than that arrived at by a more rigorous definition, involving a specified number of years in care, or limiting the category to those who have left care to become independent, without any intervening period of return to the family.

The 1991 survey (Anderson et al. 1993) found that amongst those homeless aged 16 or 17, 39 per cent had stayed in a children's home and 32 per cent with foster parents. In contrast, 18 per cent of those aged 18 to 24 had stayed in a children's home and 11 per cent with foster parents (Anderson et al. 1993). When the whole range of institutional care, including penal, psychiatric and drug and alcohol treatment establishments, was considered, it was found that the incredibly high figure of 42 per cent of homeless young people aged 16 to 24 had stayed in one or more institutions or had been fostered.

Initial research on young runaways was based on a national postal survey of chief constables, which produced the alarming estimate that 98,000 young people go missing each year in Britain (Newman 1988). This estimate should be treated with a degree of caution, however, because of problems around the definition of young runaways. Many children 'run away' from home at some point, often for very short time periods, whilst others may be reported as missing when they have not actually run away. An example of this is the relatively common situation of a young person staying with a friend or relative without making sure that their parents are adequately informed of their whereabouts. It may be supposed that the estimate of 98,000 included all of those reported as missing to the police, irrespective of the outcome of the incident.

Young people who have experience of substitute care are heavily over-represented amongst the numbers of those who have run away at some point in their lives. Just as research on youth homelessness established a strong link between homelessness and substitute care of all kinds (above), so research on young runaways has pointed even more clearly to a similar linkage. This has been successively confirmed in research studies and is now generally accepted.

Health

Some researchers have addressed the issue of the health of people who are homeless, and the 1991 survey (Anderson *et al.* 1993) found that while the majority of young people living in hostels and B&Bs were registered with a doctor, those under the age of 18 were much more likely (77%) than those aged 18 to 24 (54%) to report a health problem.

In 1999, the Social Survey Division of the Office for National Statistics carried out a survey of homeless people in Glasgow, commissioned by the Greater Glasgow Mental Health Framework Steering Group (Kershaw, Singleton and Meltzer 2000). The results were presented in an age-banded format, so it is possible to separate out a core group of young homeless people, those aged between 16 and 24. Of this age group 49 per cent were found to be suffering from some form of neurotic disorder, whilst 37 per cent routinely engaged in 'hazardous drinking' and 41 per cent admitted to some form of drug dependence. Young people in the 16 to 24 age group were less likely to report a physical illness (38%) than those in older age groups, but more likely to report a mental health problem (21%). The overall finding of the poor state of health of many homeless people, including the young homeless, may not have been altogether surprising, but this study provided a great deal of detailed information to assist in the planning of services for this group.

The existence and nature of any connection between homelessness and drug and alcohol abuse is unclear. Hutson and Liddiard (1994) stated that:

> Young homeless people are often portrayed in the media as heavy users of alcohol, and particularly drugs…there are a number of reasons why the media concentrates on these issues. Many commentators, for example, argue that the level of alcohol and drug abuse among young homeless people is greatly exaggerated. (Hutson and Liddiard 1994, p.66)

One of the difficulties in establishing or disproving any link is the level of uncertainty about drug and alcohol use in the general population of a similar age, since subjects are often unwilling to be wholly accurate about their substance use and the statistics are consequently of dubious accuracy. Hence, substance abuse by homeless young people may be merely typical for their age group (see Chapter 8 for further discussion of this issue).

Housing history and aspirations

Young people have generally been homeless for a shorter period of time than older groups of homeless people. Anderson *et al.* (1993) found that one-third of younger homeless people had been in their hostel or B&B for less than a month and nine out of ten for less than a year. On the other hand, 42 per cent of those over the age of 24 had left their last settled home more than six months earlier, compared with only 18 per cent of those aged 16 to 24. Nearly half of the younger age group (45%) said that their last settled home had been their parents' home, although 15 per cent said that their last home had been with friends or relatives, and 13 per cent considered their current B&B or hostel as being their home (Pleace and Quilgars 1999). A high proportion had left because of parental conflict (14%), relationship breakdown (6%), or abuse or violence (3%). However, 8 per cent had left to look for work, 5 per cent because of eviction and 5 per cent because of harassment in their last home. Many other social and economic factors were also cited as reasons for leaving home, showing that young homeless people become homeless for a wide variety of reasons.

However, almost all young people (95%) in the 1991 survey stated that they would have preferred to live in a house or flat and only 1 per cent wanted to return to their parents. These aspirations are reflected in every subsequent study of young homeless people, including Quarriers research (see Appendix). When the participants were asked in interview what sort of accommodation they hoped to obtain, in the future, they all wanted their own independent tenancy:

> I'd like a house in a good area and a big tall ceiling. (Young woman aged 17)

Sometimes, young people who had already spent some time in the homelessness system were willing to compromise about the location of their future home, but their desire to be the householder of their own tenancy remained undiminished:

I hope to get my own flat/tenancy, anywhere. (Young woman aged 23)

Learning points

- The proportion of young people amongst the homeless has been gradually increasing for over 20 years but young people are proportionately less likely to sleep rough than older homeless people.

- BME young people are over-represented amongst the homeless but this is more marked in the major cities of England than elsewhere. BME young homeless people are also likely to be less visible.

- Across the UK young women are slightly more likely to be homeless than young men. Information about their respective experiences of homelessness remains inconclusive, however.

- Very few young homeless people are able to obtain paid employ-ment and, in many cases, the benefits system presents real barriers to doing so.

- A high proportion of young homeless people have had a negative experience of education and find it very difficult to access the further education and training that could help them to find a path to independence.

- Between one-fifth and one-half of homeless young people have been in public care at some point. The equivalent figure for the population as a whole is around 1 per cent.

- Young homeless people are more likely than those in similar age groups in the wider community to experience a range of health problems. These include mental health difficulties and issues related to drug and alcohol use, although the evidence regarding the prevalence of drug and alcohol use amongst the homeless is unclear.

- Young people become homeless for a wide variety of reasons but almost always aspire to be a householder in their own tenancy.

Conclusion

The most striking characteristic of the single homeless generally, and young homeless people in particular, is their diversity (Kemp 1997). This heterogeneity has not been well captured in the rather simple stereotypes that have pervaded representations of homelessness in the media and in political debates. The young are the last of the subgroups within the homeless to be recognised, after the older (predominantly male) single homeless and homeless families. Data about young homeless people are correspondingly sparser. What data there are appear to show that during the last five years the numbers of young homeless people have continued to increase at a time when the numbers of all other groups of homeless people are decreasing.

Some other key characteristics are slightly clearer. Young homeless people are more likely to be in the 18 to 25 age group, than be 16 or 17. They are highly likely to be unemployed and in receipt of state benefits. Most homeless young people will have minimal educational attainments at the most basic level and no formal vocational or higher educational qualifications. A high proportion will have spent a significant proportion of their formative years in public care. A variety of physical and psychological health problems are common amongst young homeless people but there is little evidence that rates of drug and alcohol abuse are any higher than those of other young people of their age group.

Most homeless young people have been homeless for a relatively short period, usually amounting to months rather than years, and have often become homeless after leaving the parental home. Almost all young people express a desire to become economically independent and to have their own home. Their reasons for leaving home are extremely varied, and oversimplistic assumptions should be avoided at all costs.

References

Allard, A. (1996) *Youth Employment: A Contradiction in Terms*. London: Children's Centre.

Anderson, I., Kemp, P. and Quilgars, D. (1993) *Single Homeless People*. London: HMSO.

Clapham, D. and Evans, A. (2000) 'Social exclusion: The case of homelessness.' In I. Anderson and D. Sim (eds) *Social Exclusion and Housing: Context and Challenges*. Coventry: Chartered Institute of Housing.

Department of Health and Social Security (1972) *Survey of Hostels and Common Lodging Houses*. London: HMSO.

Dibblin, J. (1991) *Wherever I Lay my Hat: Young Women and Homelessness*. London: Shelter.

Fitzpatrick, S. (2000) *Young Homeless People*. Basingstoke: Macmillan.

Fitzpatrick, S., Kemp, P. and Klinker, S. (2000) *Single Homelessness. An Overview of Research in Britain*. Bristol: Policy Press.

Fitzpatrick, S., Pleace, N. and Bevan, M. (2005) *Final Evaluation of the Rough Sleepers Initiative*. Edinburgh: Scottish Executive Social Research.

Glasgow Homelessness Network (2002) *National Rough Sleeping Initiative Core Data Report, 01 April 2002–30 September 2002*. Glasgow: Glasgow Homelessness Network.

Glasgow Homelessness Network (2003) *National Rough Sleeping Initiative Core Data Report, 01 April 2003–30 September 2003*. Glasgow: Glasgow Homelessness Network.

Greve, J. (1991) *Homelessness in Britain*. York: Joseph Rowntree Foundation.

Hutson, S. and Liddiard, M. (1994) *Youth Homelessness: The Construction of a Social Reality*. Basingstoke: Macmillan.

Jackson, S. Ajayi, S. and Quigley, M. (2003) *By Degrees: The First Year. From Care to University*. London: The Buttle Trust.

Kemp, P. (1997) 'The characteristics of single homeless people in England.' In R. Burrows, N. Pleace and D. Quilgars (eds) *Homelessness and Social Policy*. London: Routledge.

Kershaw, A., Singleton, N. and Meltzer, H. (2000) *Survey of the Health and Well-being of Homeless People in Glasgow*. London: Office for National Statistics.

Lodge Patch, I.C. (1971) 'Homeless men in London:1. Demographic findings in a lodging house sample.' *British Journal of Psychiatry*, 118, 313–317.

Newman, C. (1988) *Young Runaways: Findings from Britain's First Safe House*. London: Children's Society.

Office of the Deputy Prime Minister, ODPM (2003) *Housing in Black and Minority Ethnic Communities: Review of the Evidence Base*. London: ODPM.

Pleace, N. and Quilgars, D. (1999) 'Youth homelessness.' In J. Rugg (ed.) *Young People, Housing and Social Policy*. London: Routledge.

Randall, G. (1988) *No Way Home*. London: Centrepoint Soho.

Randall, G. (1989) *Homeless and Hungry*. London: Centrepoint Soho.

Saxton, J. and Evans, E. (2002) *The Future of Homelessness? The External Environment and its Impact on Homelessness. Briefing paper on the future of homelessness as part of the London Housing Foundation's IMPACT Programme*. London: nfpSynergy.

Shelter (2005) *Young People and Homelessness*. Shelter Factsheet. London: Shelter.

Smith, J., Gilford, S., Kirkby, P., O'Reilly, A. and Ing, P. (1996) *Bright Lights and Homelessness: Family and Single Homelessness among Young People in our Cities*. London: YMCA.

Velasco, I. (2002) *I'd like to go to college. Helping Homeless Young People Access Further Education, through User Involvement*. Edinburgh: Scottish Council for the Single Homeless.

Watson, S. and Austerberry, H. (1986) *Housing and Homelessness: A Feminist Perspective*. London: Routledge and Kegan Paul.

3

A History of Youth Homelessness

The existence of many of the issues addressed by social work and social care agencies is often regarded as an inevitable part of the human condition. Poverty, disease, disability, mental ill-health and their consequences have been present throughout recorded history and seeking the ultimate eradication of these social ills seems perversely utopian. This is not the case with youth homelessness, however, since many people alive today remember a time, only 30 years ago, when the homelessness of young people was rare and viewed as shocking – an affront to the so-called civilisation of our society. This is not the case now, or at any time since the mid–late 1980s. We have become accustomed to the fact of youth homelessness and have come to regard it as an unpleasant inevitability. Whether the period prior to the 1980s, when youth homelessness was rare, was typical in the context of history is a moot point, but the fact remains that youth homelessness cannot be considered inevitable because within living memory it did not exist.

In this chapter we will briefly summarise some of the thinking about why the phenomenon of youth homelessness occurred when it did, a topic that has preoccupied many academics over a number of years. It is also important to register changes in the nature of youth homelessness and those affected by it during the years since it first occurred. Perhaps most pertinently, however, in a book with such a practical focus, we shall examine the range of social policy responses to youth homelessness and the ways in which these have changed and developed over the years.

A new problem or an old one?

During the economic depression of the late 1980s, young homeless people began to appear in numbers on the streets of British cities for the first time in a generation. Homelessness had never gone away, entirely, but had for a number of years been mainly confined to an older age group. These individuals, often referred to as 'tramps' or 'dossers', were usually male and generally assumed to be alcoholics. They were tolerated perhaps because they were not usually very visible. The 'new' phenomenon of the young homeless was greeted with shock and horror, perhaps because the economic prosperity of the period from the mid-1950s to the mid-1970s had engendered a degree of complacency amongst the population at large. Many may have thought that such distressing manifestations of public squalor had gone for good, whereas it now seems more plausible that the period marked by the absence of large numbers of homeless young people was atypical when viewed within the context of history.

A hundred years earlier, in the 1870s and 1880s, the problem of homeless and destitute children and young people on the streets of our major cities was a huge and pressing one. It provided the impetus for the development of the Christian philanthropic movement in which lie the roots of our modern voluntary sector, led by men like Thomas Barnardo in London and William Quarrier in Glasgow. There is, however, very little evidence of youth homelessness on any scale in the modern era and virtually none at all during the post-war years prior to the 1980s. One caveat should be borne in mind, however. Since local authorities had no statutory duty to regard young people who were homeless as a priority, purely on the basis of their age (see Chapter 2), throughout most of this period there was little incentive to collect data about them and the existence of the problem may have been ignored or seriously underestimated.

The UK perspective is largely the result of different aspects of homelessness having been recognised in three distinct phases, or 'waves'. Up to the early 1970s, homelessness was considered, with some justification, to have been an issue affecting mainly older single men, including many with mental health problems. Of course there were homeless people who did not conform to this stereotype but apparently not in sufficiently large numbers to warrant official recognition. During the 1970s the new phenomenon of homeless families came to light and, publicised by media activity such as the television documentary 'Cathy Come Home', formed the 'second wave'. The third and most recent wave was formed by the sudden upsurge of youth homelessness, in the late 1980s.

The genesis of the problem – why then?

An important preoccupation of early research was the need to establish the reasons for the upsurge in youth homelessness. In many studies a simple dichotomy between homelessness viewed as purely the result of the behaviour of the individual young person (individual perspectives) and homelessness as the inevitable consequence of socioeconomic forces within society (structural theories) passed for a theoretical analysis.

Individual explanations

Theorists of the 'New Right', typified by Charles Murray, linked homelessness to the concept of 'the underclass', which encompassed many disadvantaged groups within society in a fairly indiscriminate manner. According to him, the underclass in the USA was made up of a particular type of poor people, who were immersed in social problems:

> Throughout the 1970s something strange and frightening was happening among the poor people in the US. Poor communities that had consisted mostly of hardworking folks began deteriorating, sometimes falling apart altogether. Drugs, crime, illegitimacy, drop out from the job market, drop out from school, casual violence…showed large increases, focused in poor communities. As the 1980s began, the growing population of the 'other kind of poor people' could no longer be ignored and a label for them came into use. In the US, we began to call them the underclass. (Murray 1990, pp.2–3)

After visiting 'poor communities' in the UK, including Easterhouse in Glasgow, Murray concluded that a similar underclass was also arising in the UK. For Murray and his supporters, these problems resulted solely from the actions of the individuals affected, so that homelessness was seen by them as the result of the fecklessness and inadequacy of the families of origin. MacDonald (1997), however, pointed out that although underclass theory became popular from around 1987, the idea of a 'dangerous class' is much older, dating back in various forms to the Middle Ages. For Murray the three inextricably linked indicators of the underclass were crime, illegitimacy and unemployment. In his view, they were all the outcome of a process of rational choice and his preferred solution, which became very influential in both the UK and USA, was the removal of benefits from, among others, single parents. Mac-Donald (1997) argues that UK and USA positions on underclass theory diverged and that while underclass in the USA tended to mean 'race', in the UK it meant 'youth'.

The popularity of underclass theory among conservative political circles in the UK may have influenced the decision to remove state benefit entitlements from 16- and 17-year-olds, a decision which structuralists have considered one of the main causes of youth homelessness (see below). Jones (1997) goes further and argues that New Right theorists persuaded the Conservative Government to remove the welfare safety net in a vain attempt to reduce homelessness by regulating demand. If young people were leaving home and becoming homeless as a rational choice, then moving the economic goal posts so that they could only survive by remaining in the parental home would, it was argued, reduce homelessness.

There are a number of other closely related strands within the broadly individualist approaches to explaining youth homelessness. One of these, described by Hutson and Liddiard (1994) as 'The Individual Culpability Model', has much in common with underclass theory. It considers that homelessness has little or nothing to do with societal structures and is purely the consequence of young people's own behaviour. It is argued that they do not have to leave home but do so voluntarily. This perspective heavily influenced the UK Government, as evidenced by their pronouncements and policies during the late 1980s and early 1990s. These policies are now largely discredited and the aim of preventing homelessness by forcing young people to stay at home cannot be seen as a success, given the persistently high proportion of young people amongst the ranks of the homeless. A positive aspect of the individual culpability model is that it does not disempower young people and encourages the view that they are in charge of their own destiny. Perhaps for this reason it is not uncommon to hear young homeless people informally expressing views consistent with this theoretical model.

It has also been contended that the behaviour of the individual that has resulted in their homelessness is seen as a consequence of individual pathologies that in turn result from factors such as child abuse, or the experience of public care. This 'pathological model' therefore sees the causes of homelessness as rooted in the individual but, unlike the 'Individual Culpability Model', does not apportion blame. This perspective can be discerned in the attitudes of some of the agencies involved in working with the homeless, as evidenced by their reports and publications (Hutson and Liddiard 1994). It is an approach that can lead to all young people who are homeless being stigmatised as 'vulnerable' even though, in some cases, they can be shown objectively to have no serious problem other than one of accommodation.

Structural explanations

Structural explanations which located the causes of homelessness in broader social and economic structures have predominated, especially during the past ten years. Research during the 1980s and 1990s, using data from the National Child Development Survey, showed clearly that the average age of leaving home had fallen, especially with regard to those groups of young people most at risk of becoming homeless (Jones 1995). The change had been driven by economic factors and the 'at risk groups' were often the children of families of origin least able to provide ongoing support, either emotional or material.

The dominant strand within structural theory sees homelessness as a phenomenon arising from the structure of society, rather than an individual's actions or behaviour. Individual characteristics are seen as relevant only to the extent that they may explain variations in young people's vulnerability to the influence of structural forces. Hutson and Liddiard (1994) have termed this 'The Political Model', but criticise this approach on the grounds that it overlooks the importance of studying in depth the impact of structural forces in order to devise appropriate strategies to overcome the problem. The tendency of structuralists to portray homeless people as powerless victims of these forces also encourages their disempowerment and denies their capacity for self-determination. The political model has dominated thinking about the causes of homelessness, and these two criticisms go some way toward exposing the malaise that has rendered so many of the initiatives aimed at tackling homelessness ineffective.

In seeking explanations for homelessness, structuralists have looked in greater depth at various economic factors, including unemployment, low income, the effects of benefit changes, youth training and housing supply. All of these are undoubtedly relevant to the genesis of the problem but do not, on their own, provide a completely convincing explanation of why the upsurge in youth homelessness occurred when it did.

Beyond structuralism

Addressing directly the question of whether homeless people belong to the underclass, Jones (1997) offers a critique of the individualist–structuralist dichotomy and finds it wanting. She points out that the term 'underclass' was also used by structuralists and that a left–right polarisation of views could be observed. Individualists (right) tended to blame the young, whilst structuralists (left) were likely to blame the government. Craine (1997) was in many ways typical of the structuralist (left) tendency in his view of youth underclass theory, which he described as an 'ideological smokescreen', diverting attention from government culpability and presenting public issues as personal issues.

Giddens, on the other hand, suggests that people need the sense of security that is provided by rules and resources but, unlike the structuralists, believes that humans have a transformative capacity. In all but the most extreme situations, there is choice and we have the power to re-make ourselves and rebuild our social world (Giddens 1991). Viewed from this perspective, society does not determine individual behaviour, nor do individuals simply create society. In fact, both are intimately related and neither can exist independently of the other. Power is a two-way process and even those who seem to be without much power or authority, such as homeless people, have some power and ability to resist.

Many writers and researchers on youth homelessness have wrestled with the question of whether the young homeless are 'dangerous' and 'delinquent' young people, on the fringes of society, or 'victims' of circumstance, forced out of their families by the action of power structures implicit within our society. As Hall (2001) suggests in his ethnographic study of homeless youth in a British town, attempts to dichotomise these arguments are ultimately fruitless. A more informed way to understand youth homelessness is to acknowledge both of these forces at play. Young homeless people are neither the architects of their situation nor the passive objects of external forces. They are in fact both these things, attempting to find their own pathways in an environment of choice and constraint.

Early responses

There is an extensive literature concerning policy directions and the consequent patterns of service delivery relating to youth homelessness. In fact it could be argued that researchers and other writers on the topic have tended to focus on remedies to the problem, without first exploring fully its underlying causes and without really listening to the stories of those unfortunate enough to find themselves in this position. As concern about youth homelessness intensified throughout the late 1980s and early 1990s, excluded young people were increasingly seen as one of the leading social problems faced by British society. Initially, the developing services tended to concentrate on the following areas: housing need, daily living skills and employment and training.

Housing need

In view of the movements within the housing market that had contributed to the growth of youth homelessness through a shortage of affordable accommodation, there was an obvious concern to meet the housing need. Various types of accommodation were provided, including temporary and emergency accommodation and semi-independent and independent tenancies. Basic furniture and domestic equipment also had to be provided.

Daily living skills

Many young people leave their parents' home, foster home or children's home ill equipped for independent living. Many schemes have aimed to train young people in the wide variety of skills needed to run a home (Clapham and Evans 2000).

Employment and training

Many agencies have made it their priority to try to support young people's access to vocational training and eventually employment (see also Chapter 5).This focus is supported by the analysis of homelessness that regards it as a manifestation of wider economic and social exclusion (Baldwin, Coles and Mitchell 1997). According to this perspective, the most effective way of assisting a young person to find and keep their own home is to provide them with the means to earn a living.

In addition to these core areas of practice, many agencies have widened their focus to include other types of support deemed appropriate to vulnerable young people. Quilgars and Pleace (1999) identify these as social and health care needs, social needs and financial needs.

Social and health care needs

Although young people are less likely than the rest of the population to have serious health problems, homeless young people may often have had negative life experiences. These can lead to a variety of social and health problems, including mental health problems, and dependency on alcohol or drugs. If left unchecked, issues of this kind can seriously impair a young person's ability to maintain a tenancy.

Social needs

Negative life experiences can also lead to young people who are homeless becoming profoundly antisocial or withdrawn. Some services have concerned themselves with social needs, through befriending, or programmes designed to enhance the individual's social skills (Philip and Shucksmith 2004; see also Chapter 7).

Financial needs

Restricted access to benefits and difficulties in securing employment have left many homeless young people with little income. Some projects offer help to maximise and manage income to best effect in a variety of ways (Clapham and Evans 2000).

Changing patterns of need

By the 1990s a broad consensus about how to help young people in housing need was emerging:

> ...by the early 1990s, youth homelessness and the housing needs of young people were increasingly being seen as a component of a wider compound disadvantage experienced by young people from socially and economically deprived backgrounds. (Quilgars and Pleace 1999, p.110)

Within this broad range of agreed priorities for service provision, there was and still is a wide variation in the degree to which individual services are generalist or specialist and, in the latter case, the nature of the particular need that they concentrate on trying to meet.

There are no reliable estimates of the number of homeless women in the early 1970s, and the most likely reason for this is that women formed such a small proportion of those recorded as homeless by the relevant agencies that little attention was paid to them as a group. Lodge Patch's (1970) survey of the residents of two large London hostels for the homeless concerned itself solely with homeless men, making no mention of homeless women (Lodge Patch 1971). Kemp (1997) also comments that comparing the results of the 1972 and 1991 surveys, a significant increase in the proportion of women amongst the homeless was recorded. One of the principal factors bringing about this change was the impact of the Housing (Homeless Persons) Act 1977, which gave women who were homeless a statutory right to housing, provided they could demonstrate a local connection and were not 'intentionally homeless'. Initially the main beneficiaries of this change were families, so that by 1990 four out of every five homeless acceptances were households with children or where a woman was pregnant, and so the 400,000 persons accepted as homeless included approximately 200,000 children. When the third wave of homelessness (young people) arose, from the late 1980s, the gender variation was much less marked, with the number of single homeless young women equalling or exceeding that of young men.

The level of the training allowances paid to young trainees has been held down, well below the inflation rate, over many years (Coles and Craig 1999), rendering it much less likely that young people can support themselves economically. Changes in the welfare benefit system and, more specifically, the ending of state benefits for 16- and 17-year-olds, have forced young people of this age group to remain dependent on their parents. Despite the fact that the link between those changes in benefits entitlement and the growth of youth homelessness seems to have been clearly established, and despite the fact that the Conservative government that instituted those changes was replaced by a Labour administration in 1997, the restoration of benefits to 16- and 17-year-olds appears never to have been seriously considered.

Successive governments have failed to honour the 'youth training guarantee' introduced in tandem with the withdrawal of benefits, whereby all 16- and 17-year-olds not in full-time education were guaranteed a youth training place. Research undertaken since implementation of this change has shown that the guarantee has not been met, leaving a significant number of young people without support other than obscure and difficult-to-access special measures such as 'Severe Hardship Payment' (Maclagan 1993). In fact, and perhaps partly because of this, the popularity of youth training declined during the late 1980s and throughout the 1990s, to be replaced by an increasing tendency for young people to stay in education beyond the minimum school leaving age (Coles 1995).

Since winning the 1997 General Election, Labour has introduced various schemes and programmes. The most significant of these was the New Deal, which has tried to provide support for young people in finding a route out of exclusion through training and employment.

The growth of transitional support

As services for the homeless developed, transitional accommodation for young people seems to have been prioritised over other services for the same or other groups. Quilgars and Pleace (1999) showed that 34 per cent of the non-specialist beds available to homeless people in London were targeted at young people aged under 26. Most of the remaining bed spaces had no age target attached and could also be accessed by young people.

The London Hostels Directory (RIS 1998, quoted by Quilgars and Pleace 1999) lists six main categories of non-specialist transitional accommodation for homeless people:

- Direct access hostels that offer emergency places to young people in crisis.

- Low support hostels that offer only limited support, often in large premises.

- Medium support hostels, or other forms of shared accommodation, where staff are available during the day, but usually not on a 24-hour basis and where the emphasis is generally on practical support and preparation for independent living.

- Supportive hostels with a high staff/resident ratio, usually on a 24-hour basis, providing a wide range of emotional and practical support, which may well include specialist counselling.

- Foyers, or schemes that provide accommodation for young people in housing need, usually with relatively low levels of support, but directly linked to the provision of training and employment opportunities.

- Housing schemes that aim to provide good quality housing managed in a way that is supportive to young people and which either offers permanent tenancies, or a path towards eventual rehousing.

A breakdown of the figures collected in London by the Resource Information Service in 1998 also shows that young people's accommodation was largely concentrated upon transitional supported accommodation, with over 50 per cent of all low, medium and supportive schemes targeted at young people. In contrast, only 10 per cent of emergency beds and 12 per cent of housing scheme places were provided for young people.

Rough sleeping

As we have already noted (see Chapter 2), the 1991 survey on homelessness showed that rough sleeping among young people was much less common than it was in relation to older age groups of homeless people. Through the 1990s, however, concern grew that the number of young rough sleepers was increasing. There was, indeed, some evidence to support this view, but the high visibility of young people on the streets of major British cities, especially London, fuelled this growing concern. The need to end rough sleeping by young people became a major government priority and by 1998 a report by the Social

Exclusion Unit found very few under-18s sleeping rough in England, while 25 per cent of rough sleepers were aged 18 to 25 (Shelter 2005). During 2004/05 a total of 3112 people were contacted on the streets by London outreach teams and 223 of these were aged between 16 and 24 years.

In Scotland, the Rough Sleepers Initiative (RSI) was launched in 1997. It was given the target of ending the need to sleep rough in Scotland by 2003 (Saxton and Evans 2002). The final evaluation of the programme (Fitzpatrick, Pleace and Bevan 2005) found that it had generally achieved this target. Throughout its life the RSI was given the task of allocating central government funds to agencies operating projects for the homeless in many areas of Scotland. Data relating to homelessness in Scotland were collated from these agencies and published by the Glasgow Homelessness Network on a six-monthly basis.

The success of measures to greatly reduce, if not eliminate, rough sleeping by young people is clearly the major achievement of social policy in relation to this issue. It is still a matter of concern, of course, that any young person should feel it necessary to sleep on the streets. This success has also paradoxically allowed public attention to move away from the wider issue of youth homelessness and, with it, the sense of urgency about the need to achieve radical reductions in the numbers of young homeless people.

Foyers

Perhaps the single most important attempt to intervene positively in relation to this social problem under the previous Conservative administration was their support of the foyer programme which was extensively piloted during the 1990s, especially in England and Wales. This concept, originally imported from France, sought to provide accommodation, support and access to employment under one roof, within a framework that has been likened to a university hall of residence.

Unfortunately, the impact of foyers was limited during the crucial period in the 1990s, when they were being closely evaluated, by the prevailing difficulties within the employment market that they could not overcome (Anderson and Quilgars 1995). Despite the potential efficacy of the training and support on offer, there were too few suitable employment opportunities for young people. Coles took the view that:

Foyers need to become resources which young people can develop and use, not repositories into which social problems can be deposited and controlled. (Coles 1995, p.208)

In fact some of the larger supported accommodation services included in this study offered accommodation for a relatively large number of young people (39 in one case) and support services under one roof. In some cases the support was provided on a contractual basis, as is common in foyers, so that residents were obliged to utilise it as a condition of their residence, and it included support to find employment or further training. In many respects, therefore, these services could be considered foyers in all but name.

The end of hostels?

In 1991, the City of Glasgow District Council commissioned a detailed report on Robertson House, one of the seven large general hostels for the homeless that were operating within the city at that time (Wylie and Court 1991). The report was radical for its time, in that it sought the views of hostel residents as one of its principal sources of data. Although the hostel was not primarily intended for young people, the regime that allocated homeless people to it and other similar hostels did not discriminate solely on the basis of age and 9 per cent of the hostel's population was found to be between the ages of 18 and 24 years.

Wylie and Court describe Robertson House as an 'institutional building', which they define as: 'any building in which the needs of the organisation which runs it take precedence over the needs of the users who use it' (Wylie and Court 1991, p.59).

They also draw historical parallels with other institutions in which western societies have housed those considered to be 'outsiders', since the 'lazar houses' built to house lepers during the twelfth century. They asked both the residents and the staff of the hostel a series of detailed questions that suggested a real openness about the ways in which such establishments might be organised in the future. Perhaps, unsurprisingly, there was a remarkable unanimity about certain key questions, with 95 per cent of residents, for example, expressing the view that no communal space was needed in the main accommodation areas. It may seem obvious that people would not want to share any part of their living accommodation with strangers, but asking this and other similar questions and listening to the responses marked a new departure in the history of services for the homeless.

The conclusions of the study were that it was possible to redesign a large hostel of this type in a way that met the needs of residents as a complex of smaller differentiated facilities and that it was therefore possible: 'to reuse large hostels and to integrate them within an overall strategy for the de-institutionalisation of housing provision for single homeless people' (Wylie and Court 1991, p.111).

The current homelessness strategy for Glasgow (Glasgow Homelessness Partnership 2003) envisages the closure of all the remaining hostels for the homeless within the city, although some specialist units, including some of those geared to the needs of young homeless people, will probably remain in the medium–long term. Support services, even those aimed at meeting the needs of the most damaged and needy individuals, will be delivered to people in their own homes. Thus it would seem that the plan to reuse Glasgow's hostels to provide a base for non-institutional services (Wylie and Court 1991) has lasted for only 12 years and has been replaced by an unequivocal intention to close all hostels for the homeless (Glasgow Homelessness Partnership 2003).

Supported housing

Despite the concentration on transitional services throughout most of the 1990s, there were some developments in resettlement services. These generally took the form of the allocation of a support worker for a few months after a young person had been allocated their own tenancy. These services developed in response to the high levels of abandonment and other housing management problems being experienced at that time (Quilgars and Pleace 1999). Many young people who had been homeless and had passed through transitional services were being allocated their own tenancy and losing it again very quickly, often becoming homeless again and starting at the beginning of the cycle of service provision. It was not uncommon for this to happen several times to the same young person, and this 'revolving door' phenomenon became recognised as a real problem in the provision of services to young homeless people.

The most extensive study of youth homelessness in Scotland (Bannister *et al.* 1993) was commissioned by the Scottish Office's Social Work Services Group and conducted by Glasgow University. It focused on the role of social work agencies in relation to the prevention and management of the problem. Using a range of different research methods – including group interviews with homeless young people, in-depth interviews with the staff of nine participating agencies, focusing on their responses to case study 'vignettes', the monitoring of live cases over a three-month period, and a survey of policy and practice within social work and housing agencies throughout Scotland – a great deal was found to be wrong. Public services were found to have been ill prepared for the increase in youth homelessness during the late 1980s and early 1990s. Most startlingly, the relationships between agencies and homeless young people were found to have been characterised by mutual distrust. Young people tended to be suspicious of social workers in particular, whilst social workers regarded homeless young people as 'difficult cases'.

The study made a number of important recommendations for action, including an expansion of supportive accommodation and support services. It also highlighted the ineffectiveness of established social work and education services in meeting the needs of these young people and made a number of recommendations for their improvement. These included: the introduction of an 'independent living module' in schools, the development of a range of early warning 'triggers' to alert professionals to young people in crisis, the expansion of services offering mediation between young people and their parents, and the establishment of informal 'one-door' drop-in centres where young people would be less threatened than in traditional bureaucratic services and more likely to access professional help.

Services for young homeless people have suffered both from a lack of coordinated planning and a lack of agreed standards for services (Quilgars and Pleace 1999). This has arisen, in part, because of the prominent role played by voluntary sector organisations in the development and ongoing provision of services for young homeless people. Voluntary organisations have very little reason to communicate with each other and coordinate their services, especially since they have had to compete with each other for scarce resources. Bannister et al. (1993) recommended better cooperation between agencies involved in providing services for young homeless people through joint training, shared joint assessments, and better emergency liaison arrangements. A serious disparity can be discerned between services for the young homeless and other areas of social care, such as community care, in terms of the quality of joint planning and the prevalence of agreed service standards.

In recent years, however, government generally, and local authorities in particular, have taken their 'arms-length' responsibility for the determination of a coherent strategy within their area increasingly seriously. Unfortunately studies continue to record the need for more consistent inter-agency cooperation. Jackson (2002) states that:

> While there are examples of good joint working, the experience of Shelter's housing aid centres is that in many areas there has been a failure on the part of housing and social services to work together to provide services and support to vulnerable people in housing need... Joint assessments of the needs of homeless 16- or 17-year-olds provide the best opportunity to ensure clarity of responsibilities and to avoid uncertainty for young people. (Jackson 2002, p.6)

In a study of service provision for young homeless people, involving interviews with 200 homeless people in the 14 to 25 age group, in the Greater Manchester area, Reid and Klee (1999) found that: 'Overall, respondents found particular difficulties in accessing help from statutory services, such as housing and health' (Reid and Klee 1999, p.17).

Jackson (2002) claims that:

> An illustration of the difficulties is that nearly 40 per cent of young people under 19 years would have no idea where to turn if they were faced with homelessness, according to a MORI poll commissioned by Shelter. Research has also found that, although young people were more likely to have experienced problems, they are far less likely to obtain advice than their older counterparts. (Jackson 2002, p.5)

A real change in the balance of service provision came with the implementation of 'Supporting People' in 2003. This new stream of central government funding has enabled local authorities to commission and develop a large number of new services, including services for young homeless people. As the name implies, this funding stream is geared to the provision of support for people living independently, also known as 'floating support', and this has become the dominant model of service provision with small residential units providing only initial reception and assessment facilities.

In year one of the Supporting People Programme, a total of 140,207 people in Scotland were assisted by it. This equates to approximately 3.4 per cent of the adult population (Scottish Executive 2005). It is important to remember that these figures reflect the number of people using services over the course of a year and include a turnover of service users. The figures do not therefore equate with the number of service places. They also represent many different categories of need. In a survey of a sample of the 710 housing support providers on its mailing list, the Supporting People Enabling Unit (2005) found that homeless people were the primary focus of 16 per cent of providers and that young people were the main focus of 10 per cent. No figures are available for young homeless people and the total number supported in this category cannot currently be deduced.

Unfortunately, the implementation of 'Supporting People' has been exceedingly complex and difficult for providers. Furthermore, standstill budgets were imposed in years two and three and the Supporting People Enabling Unit found that:

> So far, 9 per cent of services have been offered an increase in contract value. Most services look to be offered standstill funding for the second year running. This is having an impact on the way providers view entering into three-year Supporting People contracts... The providers that do not feel confident about entering into a three-year contract cited finance as their main concern. (Supporting People Enabling Unit 2005, p.3)

Learning points

- Youth homelessness is an old problem which disappeared during the years of post-war prosperity and suddenly reappeared during the late 1980s.

- Most theorists looking for the causes of youth homelessness have blamed either the individual or the state.

- In fact, whilst government policy with regard to benefits entitlement, etc. places severe constraints on the individual, along with various forms of social exclusion, young people still have some freedom to act within these constraints.

- Social policy responses were initially dominated by simple, practical forms of support.

- The emphasis switched to the provision of transitional accommodation of various kinds during the 1990s as rough sleeping by young people appeared to be on the increase. These measures have been successful in reducing, if not eliminating, rough sleeping by young people.

- Foyers, which combined accommodation, training, employment and ongoing support under one roof, were extensively piloted during the 1990s. They were not wholly successful, mainly due to the comparative scarcity of employment opportunities at that time.

- Many local authorities have now embarked upon a policy of closing down their hostels for the homeless and replacing them with support delivered to individuals in their own tenancies.

- The development of housing support services were kick-started by the introduction of 'Supporting People', a new government funding stream. It has now been subject to some retrenchment, limiting the potential development of these services.

Conclusion

A great deal of the published literature on youth homelessness, since it became an important public issue in the 1980s, has concerned: definitions of homelessness, its causes, services to provide effective help to its casualties, and policy responses aimed at preventing homelessness in the future. None of these policy responses can claim to have been totally successful in that the available evidence points to a continuing increase in the numbers of young homeless people at a time when every other category of homelessness is reducing. Although the structural analysis contained within most of the published research on the issue has been helpful in identifying the role of the Thatcherite experiment of the 1980s in creating the phenomenon, and the sorts of state measures that might encourage or discourage homelessness, it has not provided the answer to present and future manifestations of the problem. This in part reflects the limitations of state power in resolving social and individuals' needs. The ability of homeless individuals and groups to annex and utilise discrete areas of power on their own and others' behalf must be central to any future policy agenda aimed at addressing the needs of the homeless.

Only recently have researchers and policy makers begun to pay serious attention to the experiences of young homeless people from their own perspective and to try to learn from them how more effective responses might be constructed. We knew, some years ago, that negative experiences of family life and extreme forms of family breakdown played a major part in driving young people onto the streets and we also knew that dislocation and stigma play their part so that young people tend to lose contact with old friends whom they grew up with and substitute such established relationships with 'the camaraderie of adversity' that inevitably develops between homeless people.

Published work to date has not, by and large, examined in any depth the merits of the various informal support networks available to young people who are homeless, although the Quarriers research on which this book draws (see Appendix) did try to rectify this deficiency to a limited extent. There has therefore been little consideration of how such networks might be strengthened, if such action is deemed appropriate, and whether they can contribute meaningfully to the process of inclusion in the eyes of either the professional community or of young homeless people themselves.

References

Anderson, I. and Quilgars, D. (1995) *Foyers for Young People: Evaluation of a Pilot Initiative.* York: Centre for Housing Policy.

Baldwin, D., Coles, B. and Mitchell, W. (1997) 'The formation of an underclass or disparate processes of social exclusion? Evidence from two groupings of "vulnerable youth".' In R. MacDonald (ed.) *Youth: The Underclass and Social Exclusion.* London and New York: Routledge.

Bannister, J., Dell, M., Donnison, D., Fitzpatrick, S. and Taylor, R. (1993) *Homeless Young People in Scotland: The Role of the Social Work Services.* Edinburgh: HMSO.

Clapham, D. and Evans, A. (2000) 'Social exclusion: The case of homelessness.' In I. Anderson and D. Sim (eds) *Social Exclusion and Housing: Context and Challenges.* Coventry: Chartered Institute of Housing.

Coles, B. (1995) *Youth and Social Policy. Youth Citizenship and Young Careers.* London: UCL Press.

Coles, B. and Craig, G. (1999) 'Excluded youth and the growth of begging.' In H. Dean (ed.) *Begging Questions: Street Level Economic Activity and Social Policy Failure.* Bristol: Policy Press.

Craine, S. (1997) 'The black magic roundabout. Cyclical transitions, social exclusion and alternative careers.' In R. MacDonald (ed.) *Youth, Underclass and Social Exclusion.* London and New York: Routledge.

Fitzpatrick, S., Pleace, N. and Bevan, M. (2005) *Final Evaluation of the Rough Sleepers Initiative.* Edinburgh: Scottish Executive Social Research.

Giddens, A. (1991) *Modernity and Self-identity: Self and Society in the Late Modern Age.* Cambridge: Polity Press.

Glasgow Homelessness Partnership (2003) *Strategy for the Prevention and Alleviation of Homelessness in Glasgow, 2003–2006.* Glasgow: Glasgow Homelessness Partnership.

Hall, T. (2001) *Better Times than This: Youth Homelessness in Britain.* London: Pluto Press.

Hutson, S. and Liddiard, M. (1994) *Youth Homelessness: The Construction of a Social Reality.* Basingstoke: Macmillan.

Jackson, A. (2002) 'Housing for young people: New developments in legislation, ways of working and prevention.' *Housing Care and Support 54*, 4–7.

Jones, G. (1995) *Leaving Home.* Buckingham: Open University Press.

Jones, G. (1997) 'Youth homelessness and the underclass.' In R. MacDonald (ed.) *Youth, the Underclass and Social Exclusion.* London: Routledge.

Kemp, P. (1997) 'The characteristics of single homeless people in England.' In R. Burrows, N. Pleace and D. Quilgars (eds) *Homelessness and Social Policy.* London: Routledge.

Lodge Patch, I.C. (1971) 'Homeless men in London: 1. Demographic findings in a lodging house sample.' *British Journal of Psychiatry 118*, 313–317.

MacDonald, R. (1997) 'Dangerous youth and the dangerous class.' In R. MacDonald (ed.) *Youth, the Underclass and Social Exclusion.* London: Routledge.

Maclagan, I. (1993) *Four Years' Severe Hardship: Young People and the Benefits Gap.* London: COPYSS.

Murray, C. (1990) *The Emerging British Underclass.* London: Institute of Economic Affairs.

Philip, K. and Shucksmith, J. (2004) *Supporting Vulnerable Young People. Exploring Planned Mentoring Relationships.* CRFR Research Briefing 19. Edinburgh: Centre for Research on Families and Relationships.

Quilgars, D. and Pleace, N. (1999) 'Housing and support services for young people.' In J. Rugg (ed.) *Young People, Housing and Social Policy.* London and New York: Routledge.

Reid, P. and Klee, H. (1999) 'Young homeless people and service provision.' *Health and Social Care in the Community 7*, 1, 17–24.

Saxton, J. and Evans, E. (2002) *The Future of Homelessness? The External Environment and its Impact on Homelessness.* Briefing paper on the future of homelessness as part of the London Housing Foundation's IMPACT programme. London: nfpSynergy.

Scottish Executive (2005) *Helping Homeless People. Homelessness Statement.* Ministerial statement on abolition of priority need by 2012. Edinburgh: Scottish Executive.

Shelter (2005) *Young People and Homelessness.* Shelter Factsheet. London: Shelter.

Supporting People Enabling Unit (2005) *A Report on Providers' Experience of the Supporting People Programme.* Edinburgh: Supporting People Enabling Unit.

Wylie, G. and Court, I. (1991) *Signposts. Learning from Robertson House Residents.* Glasgow: Glasgow District Council.

4

Geographical Distribution of Youth Homelessness

Just as we learned in Chapter 2 that young homeless people are not a homogenous group, so must we now look for evidence as to how youth homelessness impacts variably in different geographical locations. We will consider widely differing areas within the UK and also try to set youth homelessness within a wider international context. Any conclusions must be tentative at best, however, since the necessary data are often not available or, if they are available, are not in a form that permits direct comparison.

Nevertheless, it is instructive for those working with young homeless people and those engaged in policy formation to reflect upon the possible universal nature of youth homelessness and whether we can learn from the policy and service responses of those working in other regions or other countries.

The distribution of young homeless people across the UK

According to the best available estimates, regional levels of homelessness across England vary widely. They are highest per thousand in London, second highest in the West Midlands and lowest in Yorkshire and Humberside. These statistics are drawn from a report from Crisis (Crisis Campaigns 2001, as cited by Saxton and Evans 2002) which suggests that there might be a total of around 400,000 hidden homeless.

In 2004/05, 10,560 homeless young people were accepted by local authorities across the UK with a priority need for rehousing due to their age. Little purpose would be served by breaking this figure down by local authority area, however. It not only excludes those found to be homeless but deemed not to have a priority need for housing (see Chapter 2), but also underestimates the number actually housed. This is because some young people would have been housed on the basis of priority need justified by factors other than age, such as mental or physical health problems, or because they already had children of their own.

Efforts have been made to record data which would provide an estimate of the number of people sleeping on the streets on any given night, first by the Rough Sleepers Initiative (RSI) and more recently by the Social Exclusion Unit. The RSI operated in London from 1990 to 1999 and was launched in Scotland in 1997; formally ending in 2003. Although it is perfectly possible to compare the statistics from different local authority areas, we already know that young people are much less likely to sleep rough than older homeless people and that a great deal of youth homelessness is 'hidden' from the relevant agencies.

There are also variations in the geographical distribution of young people who are homeless with regard to their ethnic origin and gender. Hence young homeless people in Glasgow are likely to be white, whereas in many other UK cities they are somewhat more likely to be of black or Asian origin. This is not surprising, since Glasgow has a much smaller proportion of people of black and Asian ethnic origin within its population than London and many other British cities.

Glasgow's situation is also useful in highlighting differences in gender distribution. A study comparing seven British cities and four London boroughs (Smith et al. 1996) showed that just over half of the homelessness presentations in Glasgow, in the 16 to 25 age group, were young men whilst in most other cities the majority of young homeless people recorded were women. Glasgow also had the highest proportion of homeless young women who were single (61%) and the lowest proportion who were single parents (25%).

The urban 'pull'

It seems undeniable that youth homelessness is a much bigger problem in London and our major cities than it is in small towns and rural areas. This begs a number of questions, however. Are the young people who are homeless in the city merely more visible? Do they originate from the city where they are homeless and, if not, where do they come from and how did they get there? When youth homelessness first emerged in the late 1980s a great deal of the initial research explored the situation in London rather than any other part of the country. It is understandable that the nation's capital should be the focus of concern, especially since there was evidence that it had acted as a magnet to young people, especially young people from Scotland, and also had the largest population of young homeless people in the UK. Findings indicated that young people's motives for moving to London were more often prompted by 'pull' factors, such as improved employment or career prospects (46%), than 'push' factors, such as breakdown of relationships in the home (15%) (Shelter 1991). This is not to imply that young people were leaving home and making themselves homeless voluntarily for reasons of self-interest, as has sometimes been alleged. It relates to the specific motivations of young people moving to London where, more often than not, they became homeless. It seems clear that to varying extent during the last 25 years, there has been a misapprehension amongst young people that the capital represented personal opportunity of various kinds and was hugely attractive for this reason.

Dominated as it was by economic migration, the southward flow was slowed by the economic recession that affected the Southeast particularly severely between 1990 and 1992. Nevertheless the high proportion of homeless young Scots in London continued to be a source of concern throughout the subsequent decade. Although the proportion of young homeless people in the West End of London who originated from outside the capital decreased significantly during the 1990s, North–South migration began to pick up again between 1998 and 2006 and this may have had the effect of driving up homelessness in the South once again (Fitzpatrick, Kemp and Klinker 2000).

Many rural areas suffer a shortage of affordable housing. The stock of socially rented housing is often disproportionately smaller than in cities and there is also competition for the available stock from other groups, including commuters, second home-owners and retired people. While some young people may continue to move to urban centres as a matter of choice in an attempt to better themselves, as described above, there is some evidence to suggest that rural homelessness may lead some young people to move to towns and cities to find accommodation. A survey found that 40 per cent of rural districts had no emergency accommodation at all for young people and 70 per cent of rural local authorities use bed and breakfast accommodation to house homeless young people (Centrepoint and The Countryside Agency 2002).

International perspectives on social exclusion

In recent years, much attention has been directed to the processes of social exclusion, of which homelessness is an extreme example. The concept of social exclusion first emerged in French policy debates about groups at the margins of society in the 1950s. The parallel concepts of 'new poverty' and 'underclass' emerged in Britain and the USA respectively at about the same time (Edgar, Doherty and Mina-Coull 1999). Three forms of social exclusion are recognised by the European Union (EU) within its policies: economic exclusion (poverty), exclusion from the political process and exclusion from the cultural arena. Homelessness has been identified as the most extreme manifestation of social exclusion.

The European Observatory on Homelessness researches homelessness in its member states on behalf of the EU, acting on behalf of the Fédération Européenne d'Associations Nationales Travaillant avec les Sans-Abri (FEANTSA). During the mid-1990s, approximately three million people in the 15 EU countries were found to have no fixed home of their own. A further 15 million people lived in substandard or overcrowded accommodation (Edgar *et al.* 1999). FEANTSA adopts a broadly structural approach to the causes of exclusion and homelessness, focusing on varying state policies on housing and welfare:

> The failure of the respective welfare and housing regimes, subject to intense external economic and sociodemographic pressures, to effectively deliver social services creates problems of social exclusion. (Edgar *et al.* 1999, p.21)

Tosi (1996) highlights the growing importance that housing factors have in social exclusion. The importance that a home has, as a symbolic and tangible representation of 'belonging', inevitably makes homelessness the most extreme expression of social exclusion. Tosi also observes that the homeless communicate the risk of exclusion strongly because of their high visibility.

The fact that there are common problems among nations does not necessarily lead to common solutions, and the transfer of housing and planning concepts from one country to another often fails to generate the intended benefits (Daly 1996). Nevertheless, a number of significant similarities can be discerned between Britain, the USA and Canada, which are linked by broad social and economic trends. During the 1980s and early 1990s, the political leaders of the three countries – Thatcher, Major, Regan, Bush and Mulroney – saw themselves as having a common cause in seeking to cut social spending and to rein in the expansion of the welfare state.

Youth homelessness in other countries

Research on the development of youth homelessness in other economically developed countries shows a broadly similar pattern to that in the UK. There are some significant variations in numbers, but these may be largely accounted for by differences in definitions. Hence, approximately 7 persons per 1000 in Britain are accepted as being homeless by local authorities but in Canada approximately 5 persons per 1000 use the emergency shelter system, whilst in the USA about 1.5–2.5 persons per 1000 are judged to be absolutely or temporarily homeless (Daly 1996).

A comparison between Ireland and Victoria, Australia registered strong similarities between the situations in those countries and that in the UK in terms of the metropolitan focus and analysis of causation (Hayes and O'Neill 2002). Edgar et al. (1999) counsel caution with regard to data sources on homelessness across the EU, arguing that the EU countries fall into five groups, which range from no reliable primary data sources to a comprehensive national survey on homelessness that pools information from multiple sources. Even where data are extensively collected (e.g. Sweden), diversity in the type and range of data gathered limits the validity of transnational comparisons.

A link between homelessness and the inability of young people to secure unemployment has been observed in other countries as well as in the UK. Writing about the situation in Australia, Bessant (2001) comments:

> The restructuring of the labour market and economy plus the collapse of the full-time youth labour market have been accompanied by a range of specific anxieties about young people, among them youth unemployment, youth homelessness, youth suicides, juvenile delinquency and drug addiction. (Bessant 2001, p.32)

In a study of the perceptions of service providers for young homeless people in Los Angeles County, USA, employment issues rated third of all the issues identified as affecting homeless youth, with 63 per cent of young people affected. Only family relationships (86%) and housing (85%) rated higher.

Edgar *et al.* (1999) also confirm that in all countries homeless people who remain outside the institutional framework of services are hidden from official statistics. While comparisons of homelessness between economically developed countries, where there is a well-established state welfare system, are extremely difficult, as outlined above, the transferability of findings from countries where these conditions do not apply is even more dubious. This means that any comparison between the UK and any country outwith Western Europe, North America and Australasia, in terms of data, policy or services, is probably best avoided altogether.

The right to a home, though recognised by the state throughout the western world, may not exist in any real sense in many countries in the Southern Hemisphere and the Far East. In Russia, where many remnants of socialist bureaucracy coexist alongside a free market economy, the right to housing and most welfare benefits depends not only upon proof of need but also on possession of the 'propiska' or residence permit. This is a stamp inside an individual's passport and marks both the person's legal domicile in Russia and the right of that person to reside there. Lack of a propiska for the relevant town or city may in itself disqualify a person from access to housing and therefore act as one of the main causes of homelessness. Furthermore, once a person has become homeless, the lack of a propiska may also disqualify them from any form of welfare relief, even access to the ubiquitous soup kitchen (Caldwell 2004).

Services in other countries

The pattern of service provision in other countries varies greatly and is influenced by the development of different strands of policy related to both housing and welfare, as well as the place that homelessness occupies in the national culture. Daly (1996), for example, points out that in the USA and Canada emergency shelters for the adult single homeless ('the hobo') have traditionally been given priority, whilst in the UK homeless families have been accorded greater attention. There is no evidence of priority being given to the needs of young homeless people in any of the transnational studies addressing the issue of services in the EU and other western nations.

In the less economically developed countries of the world, nothing can be taken for granted in relation to welfare or housing services of any kind for those in need, including young homeless people. In Russia's postsocialist society, for example, all-encompassing state provision has been replaced so far only by charitable relief efforts of the crudest kind, such as the soup kitchen. Melissa Caldwell's ethnographic study of poverty and social welfare in Moscow during the 1990s (Caldwell 2004) shows how the poor, including the homeless, use improvisational tactics to satisfy their material needs, while social support has been developed to a high level through networks of informal relationships. Caldwell cites many examples of inspiring and sometimes ingenious mutual aid and self-help and it might be held that these challenge prevailing ideas about the role of the state in relation to poverty and welfare. On the other hand, there is little evidence that such creativity can be promoted in a welfare state environment and it may be that it can only develop as a survival mechanism in the absence of universal state welfare provision.

Germany has been the most successful of all Western European countries in restricting youth unemployment. Around two-thirds of those young people on the job market receive apprenticeship training which has sufficiently high status to attract young people because of real and perceived benefits (Allard 1996). On-the-job training is combined with academic study and certification of apprenticeships and leads to advantages in the job market. The training is specific enough to prepare young people for highly skilled occupations while also providing a broad foundation that can aid career mobility. The programme costs employers more than they gain and there is no guarantee that the apprentice will stay on once he or she is trained. Employers still participate, however, because the system ensures a supply of skilled workers.

Learning points

- There are wide variations in the numbers and characteristics of young homeless people in different parts of the UK.

- Because of the hidden nature of much youth homelessness and difficulties in data collection, accurate estimates of numbers are difficult to arrive at (as discussed in Chapter 1).

- There are also variations across the UK in the proportion of young homeless people from black and minority ethnic backgrounds and in the gender distribution.

- Youth homelessness appears to be primarily a phenomenon of our major cities. This is largely because of the 'pull' they exert for mainly economic reasons but also because of the availability of services in the cities.

- Young people are also homeless in smaller towns and rural areas.

- Broadly similar trends with regard to homelessness can be discerned in other developed western nations, with homelessness recognised as one of the most extreme manifestations of social exclusion.

- Differences in the nature and level of data collected make detailed comparisons between countries almost impossible.

- Youth homelessness in countries where there is no highly developed state welfare system may take radically different forms.

- Similarly there are wide variations in the level and type of services for young homeless people in other countries. Whilst we can undoubtedly learn much from their experience, caution should be exercised over detailed comparisons and generalisations.

Conclusion

Only when youth homelessness becomes a visible public phenomenon do the general public become aware of it. When homeless young people appear on the streets they provoke widespread shock and sympathy, at least in western democracies with highly developed welfare provision. This only happens, however, when those welfare services break down or are overwhelmed by demand. At other times, youth homelessness is largely hidden from public view, but no less damaging and wasteful of individual potential. This generalisation seems broadly true across the UK and in other welfare states, despite many local variations.

It is almost impossible to quantify this hidden aspect of homelessness and therefore to plan for future services to deal with the problem. Even where data collection is sophisticated and standardised nationally, it rarely permits safe international comparisons. A great deal of the information that is collected is concerned with evaluating the impact, or otherwise, of government policy initiatives and can be very detailed. If we are to achieve significant reductions in the numbers of young people experiencing homelessness, it will probably be necessary to simplify, standardise and de-politicise the collection of relevant data.

References

Allard, A. (1996) *Youth Employment: A Contradiction in Terms.* London: Children's Centre.

Bessant, J. (2001) 'From sociology of deviance to sociology of risk. Youth homelessness and the problem of empiricism.' *Journal of Criminal Justice 29,* 31–43.

Caldwell, M.L. (2004) *Not by Bread Alone: Social Support in the New Russia.* Berkeley: University of California Press.

Centrepoint and the Countryside Agency (2002) *Youth Homelessness and Social Exclusion in Rural Areas. Rural Affairs Briefing 2002.* London: Centrepoint and the Countryside Agency.

Daly, G. (1996) *Homeless. Policies, Strategies and Lives on the Street.* London: Routledge.

Edgar, B., Doherty, J. and Mina-Coull, A. (1999) *Services for Homeless People: Innovation and Change in the European Union.* Bristol: Policy Press.

Fitzpatrick, S., Kemp, P. and Klinker, S. (2000) *Single Homelessness: An Overview of Research in Britain.* Bristol: Policy Press.

Fitzpatrick, S., Pleace, N. and Bevan, M. (2005) *Final Evaluation of the Rough Sleepers Initiative.* Edinburgh: Scottish Executive Social Research.

Hayes, T. and O'Neill, D. (2002) 'Homelessness, the state and the third sector: Comparative perspectives from Ireland and Victoria, Australia.' Edinburgh: University of Edinburgh. Inpublished.

Saxton, J. and Evans, E. (2002) *The Future of Homelessness? The External Environment and its Impact on Homelessness.* Briefing paper on the future of homelessness as part of the London Housing Foundation's IMPACT programme. London: nfpSynergy.

Shelter (1991) *Living on the Borderline: Homeless Young Scots in London.* London: Shelter.

Smith, J., Gilford, S., Kirkby, P., O'Reilly, A. and Ing, P. (1996) *Bright Lights and Homelessness: Family and Single Homelessness among Young People in our Cities.* London: YMCA.

Tosi, A. (1996) 'The excluded and the homeless: The social construction of the fight against poverty in Europe.' In E. Mingione (ed.) *Urban Poverty and the Underclass: A Reader.* Cambridge, MA: Blackwell.

5

Something to Do

Education, Training and Employment

Casual observers of young homeless people, particularly the less sympathetic amongst them, have often been led to ask 'why don't they get jobs?' This is a perfectly reasonable question because, if they were able to find and maintain paid employment, the economic independence that accompanies even low-paid work would surely enable these young people to escape from homelessness with only minimal assistance from others. Privately rented accommodation would become an option and, although the need for a substantial rent deposit might still pose a problem, a range of informal arrangements, whereby individuals share accommodation and expenses with others in a similar position, would be possible. This presupposes the availability of a disposable income, however, and the most common route to such an income is through employment.

In fact, as we have already established, very few young homeless people have jobs (seee Chapter 2).

In this chapter we shall consider why this is the case and what can be done about it. We shall also examine how young people can be helped to become active in the labour market through education, training and other personal development programmes. As the title of the chapter implies, young people often regard these activities as little more than a way of passing the time but they are, of course, much more than that. Acquiring the skills and knowledge to equip an individual to pursue his or her chosen career path is just as vital for a young person who is homeless as it is for a young person living at home and applying for university, if not more so.

Aspirations

Before going any further, however, perhaps we should deal with the question of whether homeless young people really want to work or have any expectation of doing so. Almost all the young people involved in the Quarriers research (see Appendix) echoed the sentiments of a 20-year-old young man when he said:

> I need a job or some kind of training to keep myself occupied.

In the Quarriers research, those who completed an interview were also asked what type of job they hoped to do in the future (see Table 5.1). It may be surprising that a very wide variety of possible career options was recorded. These ranged from the relatively unambitious, such as 'Cleansing Department', 'working on a building site' and 'anything', to occupations requiring lengthy periods of full-time study and training, including 'civil engineer', 'computer programmer/analyst' and even 'environmental toxicologist'. In fact, they were like any other sample of young people of this age group, in that many had high ideals and aspirations with regard to future careers.

Table 5.1 Career aspirations of young people in the Quarriers research

Subject	Gender	Career goal
1	F	No interview
2	F	Childcare or cooking
3	F	No interview
4	M	Cleansing Department
5	F	Work with the homeless drug and alcohol users
6	F	Unspecified
7	F	No interview
8	F	Counsellor

Table 5.1 continued

Subject	Gender	Career goal
9	M	No interview
10	M	Unspecified
11	M	Unspecified
12	M	Civil engineer
13	F	A nanny or a lawyer
14	F	Caring for people
15	F	Computer programmer/analyst
16	M	Computer engineering
17	M	Working on a building site
18	F	Interior designer, or carer for people with special needs
19	M	Carpenter/joiner
20	M	Lifeguard, pool assistant, or fitness instructor
21	F	No interview
22	F	Nursery teacher
23	M	'Anything'
24	M	Environmental toxicologist
25	M	Construction worker or van person
26	F	Childcare or social care
27	F	Work with children in care
28	M	Work with the elderly
29	M	Joiner
30	M	Unspecified
31	F	Paramedic, or streetworker with homeless people

The likelihood of these young people achieving their career goals, or even retaining the high aspirations they may once have had, is a different matter entirely. Roberts (1993) argues that disadvantaged young people like these will eventually be socialised by their experiences towards acceptance of more menial roles. He maintains that these 'lesser' career paths were always inevitable, having been determined by their social class and family background. It is difficult to argue against this view without the benefit of foresight or at least a long-term follow-up study, but the belief that such a downwardly mobile future is completely predetermined is ultimately a negative and disempowering viewpoint.

One way of retaining the positive outlook that is so important when working directly with young people is to keep in mind examples of those who have succeeded despite all the odds. Like any other form of disadvantage, homelessness does spur a minority on to solid achievements. A young woman prominently involved in the Quarriers research whose ambition was 'a job caring for people' successfully completed an HNC qualification in social care and applied for a job as a care assistant in a home for the elderly. Over a year later, she wrote to one of the researchers:

> I got the job and I'm now still working there. However, now that I have more experience, I am now looking for another job that will be more challenging and BETTER PAID… Things have been really good for me, just now. I have a really nice flat and have made loads of friends at work.

Whilst young people like the young woman quoted above frequently buck the trend, they do so in the face of significant disadvantage.

Barriers to employment and training

Many young homeless people express a fairly negative view of the training and further education opportunities available to them:

> I started a New Deal. Two weeks, it lasts, walked to it with M, sat in a room with other people. Was bored out my face. (Young woman aged 19)

Others, however, do find the motivation to make use of opportunities that are potentially open to all in the community:

> Aye I'm goin tae college in August. I'm might dae computing or something. I don't know yet. (Young man aged 20)

A minority may already have experienced positive help from various agencies and individuals and be able to acknowledge the assistance they have received. A young woman aged 21, in answer to a question about experiences of various sources of help whilst homeless, and their relative merits, said:

> Agency X. Volunteer work placement working with disabled people on a community basis. Got my college course because a member of staff dealing with employment, FE from the hostel helped me access college. Agency X was a brilliant organisation, friendly, and I still keep in contact with workers from there.

It seemed that, in the eyes of many, neither open access to community facilities nor specially targeted programmes were enough. They wanted training and education to be built into the hostel regime itself, and the same young woman (above) was asked whether she had enough activities to keep her interested and busy during the day. She responded:

> I used to, half because I had college, feeling pure irritated and stuck in hostel all day – brain damaged! Because I've stayed in Agency X so long there's lots of people I am sick of. I would like to access teachers providing activities, e.g. guitar. Staff should have various talents which they can teach us, e.g. art lessons, music, singing, cooking sessions, etc. to keep us occupied.

Part of the Quarriers research involved asking a large group of agencies whose remit involved service provision to the homeless whether they felt that young people using their services had access to an adequate range of employment opportunities, training and other purposeful day activities. Of the 58 responders, 36 addressed this question and were equally divided, 18 replying 'yes' and 18 'no'. Those that had replied negatively were asked what types of activities were missing, or in short supply. Many focused on the need for better support networks to help vulnerable young people to access mainstream opportunities which they often found intimidating, due to their lack of confidence and low self-esteem. Six agencies recorded the lack of jobs and apprenticeships, other than low paid ones in the retail and commercial sector. A shortage of opportunities for young women and for black and minority ethnic (BME) young people was also mentioned.

Agencies were fairly equally divided on their view of the proportion of young people making full use of existing services, with one responding 'all' and a further 12 replying 'many'. On the other hand, six agencies thought that about half of their young people took up such activities to the fullest extent and 16 thought that 'few' were able to achieve such a high level of take-up.

Personal problems and deficiencies, on the one hand, and structural issues, on the other, were both cited as barriers to opportunity. Surprisingly, however, the balance fell very much on the side of personal barriers, which were mentioned by almost every agency responding to this question. 'Lack of confidence' was highlighted by nine agencies, whilst another nine mentioned, 'lack of motivation' and six thought that 'substance misuse issues' created a significant barrier. Other personal factors specified by more than one respondent included: 'lack of interest' (5), 'erratic lifestyles' (5), 'mental health issues' (3) and 'emotional difficulties' (2). Structural issues highlighted as barriers included: 'inaccessibility' (5), 'lack of crèche/ nursery placements' (2) and 'lack of support' (2).

A subset of 12 agencies, whose primary remit involved working with young homeless people, provided some thoughtful analysis. Prompted by the same question, one wrote:

> The main reason is the current homeless situation of the young people and the fact they are only here for a very short time, before going anywhere in the city. This makes local employment/training difficult to sustain; also it is a confusing and stressful time for many who are homeless for the first time. The range of young people can make other activities difficult at times due to the mix of people with difficult behaviours/addiction problems etc.

Another agency supplied the following list of barriers that were seen as significant:

> Childcare difficulties (i.e. nursery hours); chaotic situations (not used to having a structured day); appointments with other professionals, relating to housing, children, etc.

Perhaps the greatest barriers to employment, however, arise from the mechanism whereby services are funded and its relationship to any state benefit to which a young person might be eligible. Almost all transitional housing services in the UK are funded at present through Housing Benefit and Supporting People. Most individual Housing Benefit entitlement is claimed directly by the service on the person's behalf, but once they enter employment this entitlement is greatly reduced and they become eligible to pay a large proportion of their living expenses from their wages. The jobs that most young people can realistically expect to secure are likely to be relatively low-paid so the benefit to them, in terms of disposable income – money that they can actually spend – is minimal. When one considers the difficult bureaucratic process involved in securing or changing benefit entitlements with changing circumstances, the prevailing system not only offers no incentive for young people in this situation to work, it also acts as a positive disincentive.

Furthermore, the rules regarding disregarded income for recipients of various state benefit streams have been tightened over the years to the point where even minimal rewards from a few hours of work experience must be declared and will affect benefit levels. When the bureaucratic factor is considered, it is understandable that paid work is simply not on the agenda for most young people until after they have escaped from homelessness. This is regrettable because paid employment could, in other circumstances, form one of the most powerful motivators to young people who need to engage actively with the difficulties they face in order to achieve the lifestyle they desire.

Of course, as we shall see, there is still much that can be done, particularly in terms of training and education, but the financial motive, so vital to most of us in seeking to better ourselves, is largely absent.

Homeless and still at school

It is now the norm for young people to remain in full-time education beyond the age of 16. Young people becoming homeless, whilst still attending school, might more commonly be accommodated by the local authority, but it is not unknown for them to find their way to services for the homeless. One of the 31 young people involved in the Quarriers research was in this situation and her own wishes and best interests suggested that she should be supported to continue to attend school from the hostel for young homeless people where she temporarily lived. She was a promising student who had good academic prospects and was studying for exams at the time when she was made homeless. In fact the staff of the hostel supported her as best they could, although the hostel environment and regime were far from ideally suited to a young person in this situation.

This example is mentioned to illustrate the dangers of assuming that all homeless young people conform to the same 'identikit' description.

Whilst the majority may have become alienated from education at an earlier stage of their lives and have few prospects and little interest in conventional achievement, a significant minority may be in a very different situation and it is the responsibility of the staff of the relevant services to use all their skills and ingenuity to respond effectively to individual need, however far from the 'mainstream' it might seem.

The wider policy context

The employment of school leavers in the UK has been marginalised in the past 15 years. This process has been associated with a decline in the overall size of the youth labour market. Combining the effects of a decline in the birth rate and increasing participation in the educational system, the number of 16- to 24-year-olds working, or available for work, on a full-time basis, is estimated to have dropped from approximately 6.5 million in 1984 to under 4.0 million by 1998 (Brynner *et al.* 2002). The traditional 'entry jobs' for young people, such as apprenticeships for males and clerical/secretarial work for females, are declining areas of employment and have been largely replaced by poorly paid posts in the service sector. The earnings of young people relative to those over 25 years have declined dramatically, and while economic growth has brought about a general decline in unemployment since 1993, the impact among 16- to 19-year-olds has been less evident.

The approach to the problem of youth unemployment in the UK over many years has been characterised by a series of 'knee-jerk' responses rather than a long-term strategy. Hence, the last 30 years has seen the successive advent and demise of Job Creation, YTS and YT, each one prompted by a market-related crisis. The present 'Skill Seekers' and 'New Deal' programmes bask in a more favourable climate of comparatively full employment and link into a national qualification framework (NVQ/SVQ), via a twin-track approach, with colleges of further education and other training providers supporting employers. It is still, however, seen as a 'safety net' for failing pupils in transition rather than as a source of opportunity and a positive choice offering real career potential.

There is evidence of a growing disparity between those young people who gain access to and benefit from the expansion of further and higher education and those who do not (Brynner *et al.* 2002). A recent longitudinal survey of young adults, aiming to provide a comprehensive overview of youth transitions, in the West of Scotland (Furlong *et al.* 2003), found that only around 6 per cent of the total population of young people experienced chaotic transitions, characterised by high levels of unemployment. The study piloted a multidimensional model of transitions, in recognition of the complex nature of vulnerability. Although young people were often able to make up for deficits in their experience, by utilising compensatory resources, a small minority simply had no reserves to draw upon. Family support featured prominently amongst these compensatory resources, so it is easy to see how homeless young people, with their background of fractured family life, tended to fall within Furlong's 'chaotic' 6 per cent.

The concerns of young people and agencies, quoted above, reflect this polarisation in the youth labour market and the need to tackle it more effectively. It is a complex and deep-seated problem, but there is a clear need to refocus attention on these increasingly excluded young people who cannot and will not benefit from improved educational opportunities.

Furlong *et al.* (2003) conclude that initiatives such as the New Deal could be targeted more effectively and suggest three groups who would benefit from more specific interventions. These are: young people who encounter a substantial period of unemployment (six months or more) beginning in the first year of labour market entry; young people who experience cumulative unemployment of over a year, at any stage; and young people with complex career histories (even when they have managed to avoid long-term unemployment).

Local and individualised programmes of support, provided by specialised agencies, may provide part of the answer but it remains to be seen whether they will prove any more effective than large-scale state provision like New Deal. In the early 1990s the foyer pilot project emerged to try to help young people break out of the vicious circle of homelessness and unemployment by advocating an integrated approach to tackling their housing and employment problems. Seven of the early foyers were subject to an independent evaluation that monitored their progress over a 26-month pilot period (Anderson and Quilgars 1995). The study found that although the foyers provided a range of opportunities to improve young people's chances of finding employment, it was not an initiative that created any additional jobs. The pilot project was conducted at a time of recession in the labour market and the evaluation found that little could be done to counteract its effects. Further discussion of the foyer movement therefore belongs in Chapter 9.

Lifestyle and motivation

The experience of homelessness almost invariably involves an element of trauma, especially for young people. Traumatised people cannot address long-term issues, such as the need to seek and make use of opportunities that may increase their employability in the future. Even when their physical safety has been secured, most of their energies may be taken up by psychological survival, especially when they have other issues to deal with, such as addiction or mental health problems, self-harm, or offending behaviour. Hence, young people in the early crisis stages of homelessness will generally prove quite incapable of even thinking about education or training. In time, most will move beyond this phase, although there is no certainty about it and no way of knowing how long this will take. Everybody is different and deals with trauma in their own way and at their own pace. It is pointless and potentially harmful to try to force the issue. The evaluation of services must take this into account and not focus on crude statistics as indicators of 'success'.

Humans have an almost infinite capacity to adapt, however, and as young people become more settled and their temporary home starts to feel more comfortable, an increasing number of choices begin to open up for them. These will include opportunities that appear at face value to be positive, including college courses, training programmes and a variety of access and confidence building programmes. As we have already seen, a whole range of barriers, such as those specified by agencies during the Quarriers research, come into play to make what are apparently positive choices very difficult for young people to grasp. There are practical barriers, such as the need to attend regular appointments with various agencies, but I would like to suggest that the most commonly experienced of all these many barriers is low self-esteem and the fear of failure that accompanies it. These are young people who have very often failed in the past, especially in education. Even where this is not the case, homelessness itself is experienced as a failure.

It may appear that the problem that young people face in grasping these positive opportunities is primarily one of motivation. If they are pursuing a lifestyle that involves sleeping for much of the day and partying for most of the night, then it is understandable the strength of their desire to help themselves might be questioned. In some cases, motivation may indeed be lacking and, if so, workers will find themselves largely powerless to intervene. In many more cases, however, workers must look beyond the superficial and see the lack of confidence and low self-esteem that lie behind it. The best way of supporting such young people is to help them to achieve success, starting with the smallest and apparently most insignificant task which they may wish to succeed in but are afraid to try. We shall consider the practicalities of this process later in this chapter.

Learning skills

Once a young person is ready to learn, despite all of the practical and psychological barriers to learning that they may have had to negotiate, they may still lack the skills to do so. The literature on further education frequently refers to several subtly different skill sets. Three of the most common are 'Key Skills', 'Basic Skills' and 'Study Skills'. Wallace (2001) provides a helpful breakdown. The 'Key Skills' are part of the post-16 curriculum and form the subject matter of a specific qualification, which can be counted towards the entry requirements for higher education. They are communication, number and IT skills that employers also find desirable in applicants. The term 'Basic Skills', on the other hand, usually refers to reading, writing, speaking and number. Some young people, having left compulsory schooling, may not feel confident in these areas for many reasons. They may have a learning disability, have become alienated from school and/or developed a pattern of non-attendance, so that important stages in their learning have fallen within periods of absence and have never been successfully remediated. 'Study Skills' are those that students need to have in order to be able to work effectively as independent learners. They include the ability to take notes, to find information from both libraries and the internet, and to plan and utilise time efficiently.

Workers in services for young homeless people have a different function in relation to each of these types of skills. The key skills are likely to be essential for the posts that they occupy, so they should be able to model competence in them. The teaching of basic skills to adults is a specialist role and the task of the worker is to identify where young people might need help with basic skills and to ensure that they receive the appropriate specialist support if necessary. Services aimed at providing this specialist help may not be commonplace, but do exist within both the homelessness field and in the wider community. We can all provide help and guidance with study skills, however, and the encouragement and support that workers can give on note-taking, research skills and time management provides one of the most important ways in which young people can be encouraged to become effective and independent learners (Wallace 2001).

Finding the right career path

We have already seen how variable young people's career aspirations may be. Even allowing for some tongue-in-cheek bravado, it is remarkable how far they range from the highly ambitious to the completely unambitious. Disadvantage and self-perceived failure have the tendency of depressing aspirations and limiting young people's potential, but unrealistic aspirations that bear no relation to individual skills and abilities also court failure and, in the long term, only reinforce the low self-esteem that will already be hampering the progress of so many young people who find themselves homeless.

For these reasons, I advocate a 'strength-based' approach to intervention with young people. In the area of careers counselling that means finding areas of ability which the young person themselves may not have recognised or about which they may be in denial. Staff working in transitional services, especially key workers, will have good opportunities to observe young people in a wide variety of different situations, identify their strengths and interpret these back to them. Thereafter the young person can be encouraged to choose a path suited to their particular strengths and abilities and be reminded when necessary that they can succeed because these are the things that they are good at. The subsequent choice of action is, of course, entirely that of the young person and it is very possible, or even highly likely, that they will reject the kind of quasi-parental advice that I am advocating. Nevertheless, the important thing is that someone is seen to care enough to take a sufficient interest in an individual and be in a position to give such advice.

Encouragement and support

Many agencies working with young homeless people are seeking to build the kind of support that we have been discussing into their programmes in recognition of the now widely held belief that this kind of support is absolutely invaluable. It is hard to think of any form of assistance that could be more effective in helping a young person to escape from homelessness.

When agencies were asked as part of the Quarriers research what steps they were taking to overcome the various barriers to employment, education and training, a wide range of responses was supplied. At one end of the spectrum, four agencies reported that they had either implemented, or were seeking funding for, their own training/employment support initiative, usually in the form of a dedicated post. This was often in tandem with a programme of in-house activities of a broadly educational nature. One agency responded as follows:

> Seeking funding for employment/training development worker to be part of a service development team, targeting health, accommodation development, employment/training and service user participation.

Other agencies referred young people to other, more specialist, services for help and support in this area, either in addition to their own programme, or as an alternative:

> We provide our own opportunities, direct young people to [agencies specialising in the provision of day opportunities for young people], we organise outward bound excursions and preparation for independent living housing programme. Also budgeting, cooking sessions, etc.

Other respondents focused on the support, encouragement and information that they provided to help young people to overcome barriers but very little evidence was offered as to how this worked in practice. Sometimes a contract of a more or less formal nature was used to motivate young people, and one agency intimated that residents at the unit were subject to a 'requirement to attend a purposeful activity'.

Ultimately, the model by which this kind of support is delivered is not crucial. The same outcome can be achieved in a variety of ways. The vital component of service delivery is that it does not allow young people to feel that they are being written off and that nothing is expected of them, or hoped for on their behalf.

Study facilities and travel costs

Although young people in residential services for the homeless will now normally have their own single room which can be made suitable for the private study that inevitably accompanies every educational and training course, there may be obvious practical difficulties. It may, for example, be noisy or prone to frequent visits from other residents. The agency concerned may for very good reasons have decided to restrict access to computers and the internet and yet this is likely to be essential to many courses of study. If satisfactory study facilities and computer access cannot be provided within the service then steps should be taken to provide them externally.

Financial barriers can hinder progress towards independence in many ways and the high cost of public transport may be one of them. The inability to afford the cost of bus fares to and from college may be the entirely preventable reason for a young person dropping out of a course to which they were committed. Those new to further education are unlikely to be familiar with the eligible criteria and application process for various grants and bursary schemes that most local authorities have for this very purpose. Agencies should be alive to the relevance of these issues, in respect of their population of residents at any given time, and take steps to have the relevant information close at hand.

It is important that the agency takes active steps to help those young people who are committed to education or training to overcome practical barriers of this kind that could so easily upset the sometimes fragile equilibrium of their motivation.

Learning points

- Like any other young people, those who are homeless may have high aspirations, but disadvantaged people tend through time to be socialised into the acceptance of menial roles for themselves.

- Positive role models are important in motivating young people, especially those from a similar situation who have succeeded on their own terms.

- Homeless young people face many barriers to employment, education and training. Perhaps most importantly, many will have had previous negative experiences of education and this may have left them with an expectation and fear of failure.

- Employment is not a practical proposition for young people who are homeless, because of the benefits system.

- Not all young homeless people are alienated from education. Current students, including some still at school, do on occasion find their way into the homeless system.

- Homelessness almost always involves trauma, and traumatised people cannot learn. Only after the basic human needs have been satisfied can homeless young people start to address the educational and training needs that will impact on their future prospects.

- What can seem like a lack of motivation in young people is often caused by low self-esteem. A belief in their own ability to succeed, even in small things, can help to combat this.

- Even when sufficiently confident and motivated, learning still involves various skills. Workers can help young people to acquire the skills and support that they need.

- Insofar as young people are amenable to influence, they should be encouraged to follow learning and career paths that make positive use of their strengths and abilities.

- Various simple practical measures of support can easily be overlooked and may make a significant difference to young people's ability to sustain their motivation to learn.

Conclusion

It is natural to think of 'housing' as the solution to 'homelessness', and of course in a very direct and logical sense this is true, but it is by no means the whole story. A successful pathway out of homelessness involves not just a roof over one's head, but a sustainable way of life. For anyone in our society, this involves a way of making a living and a reasonably satisfying way of spending one's time. For the more fortunate amongst us, these two elements can be different parts of the same thing – a career. For many others, they may have to be addressed separately. Probably the majority of the population have to settle for a job that they do not particularly enjoy and leisure-time interests or hobbies that make life worthwhile. For the homeless, who are young and still at an early stage of reaching a conclusion on this dichotomy, the ability to find a path through which they can learn the limits of their potential and strive to reach them and a direction that utilises their strengths and abilities to best effect is absolutely priceless. There is nothing more important than this in helping homeless young people in the medium and long term and nothing should be given a higher priority.

References

Anderson, I. and Quilgars, D. (1995) *Foyers for Young People: Evaluation of a Pilot Initiative.* York: Centre for Housing Policy.

Brynner, J., Elias, P., McKnight, A., Pan, H. and Pierre, G. (2002) *Young People's Changing Routes to Independence.* York: Joseph Rowntree Foundation.

Furlong, A., Cartmel, F., Biggart, A., Sweeting, H. and West, P. (2003) *Youth Transitions: Patterns of Vulnerability and Processes of Social Inclusion.* Edinburgh: Scottish Executive Research Findings, No 8.

Pleace, N. and Quilgars, D. (1999) 'Youth homelessness.' In J. Rugg (ed.) *Young People, Housing and Social Policy.* London and New York: Routledge.

Roberts, K. (1993) 'Career trajectories and the mirage of increased social mobility.' In I. Bates and G. Riseborough (eds) *Youth and Inequality.* Buckingham: Open University Press.

Wallace, S. (2001) *Teaching and Supporting Learning in Further Education.* Exeter: Learning Matters.

6

Family

A Help or a Hindrance?

Young people become homeless for a variety of reasons, but most commonly they have left the family home at an earlier age than is typical in our society. Although there are many reasons why this occurs, family dysfunction often plays a significant part. Whilst the most common pattern of leaving home shows young people leaving and returning on several occasions, before becoming permanently settled in their own household, young homeless people frequently feel unable to return home once they have left. This may be because of poor relationships, arguments or even domestic violence between parents, or between parents and children. In some cases children may have been physically or sexually abused in the family home.

It is now rare to hear families or young people blamed for their homelessness. Perhaps because of this subtext of family conflict and tension it is, however, still quite common for professionals to regard young homeless people's families as little more than an irrelevance in the struggle that they face in establishing themselves as independent adults. The purpose of this chapter is to examine the continuing importance of family, if any, and consider whether there are continuing elements of positive family life that can be supported and encouraged. If so, is it possible that 'family', however imperfect, might still be a positive force that can be mobilised in the fight against homelessness?

Youth transitions

Traditional notions of citizenship, wherein individuals assume the full range of rights and responsibilities, rely on biological definitions as to when adulthood is attained. The twentieth century saw the developing recognition of a new life stage known as 'youth', a transitional period between childhood and adulthood. Key indicators of adulthood include living independently, economic independence, the ability to form relationships and become a parent, and independence as a consumer in the marketplace. In terms of rights, however, the legal definition of when youth ends and adulthood begins is unclear. Young people gain access to adult rights gradually, at different stages, with no overall logic or consistency. In Scotland, for example, young people are not legally entitled to drink in a public house until they are 18, but they may marry, without parental consent, at 16. Similar inconsistencies apply to different aspects of life across the UK.

Some rights are dependent on status rather than chronological age. Young people who remain in full-time education, for example, may be entitled to free prescriptions and discounted fares on public transport. In some cases, they may qualify for local authority bursaries or student loans. Young people themselves may have varying perceptions of the stage they have reached on the path to adulthood. A study of young people's health and family life asked young people themselves the question, 'Do you consider yourself to be an adult?' (Brannen *et al.* 1994, p.29). One-quarter of the respondents said that they did consider themselves adults, one-half claimed to be 'in between', and one-quarter felt that they were 'not adult'.

France concludes that 'youth is a complex term that is continually being re-defined legally and culturally at all levels of society' (France 1996, p.32). This makes it difficult to compare homeless young people's experience of family life with that of others in society. Their personal histories, however, frequently demonstrate a conundrum, in that they have been forced to leave their parental home at an early age, whilst policy developments in wider society over the last 25 years have had the effect of delaying their progress towards full citizenship and leaving them in a kind of suspended adolescence. The term 'fractured transitions' has been used to refer to situations in which young people move from one status position without managing to attain a secure, stable or positive outcome in another (Coles 1995). The term accurately describes the situation faced by many homeless young people.

Young people who are homeless do not form a homogenous group and homelessness is not a condition whereby their status can be defined other than with regard to the simple fact of whether or not they have a home. They are first and foremost young people and only secondarily homeless people. Hence they may occupy any of the rungs of the ladder that leads from childhood to adulthood, either according to their own perceptions, or the way that others define them.

Youth transition is often likened to a 'pathway' and it is rarely smooth and painless. A pathway that includes a period of homelessness along the way would generally be regarded as exceptionally rocky or 'fractured'. Of course, the young person's path through this period of transition is not entirely determined by socioeconomic factors beyond his or her control and also contains an element of choice. Choice around whether to remain in full-time education beyond the age of 16, or alternatively to enter the labour market, is real to some extent but is also influenced by a range of powerful external factors. These include whether places are available at the chosen school or college and the willingness and capability of either the state or the parents to meet the costs of supporting the young person while he or she is there. Similarly young people may only enter the labour market if employers have suitable jobs that they are willing to offer them. If these jobs are perceived by young people to be of limited value in enabling them to achieve their long-term goals, then they may 'choose' not to enter the labour market and remain in full-time education.

Moving into independent accommodation is also manifestly not only a matter of choice but also dependent on the state of the housing market. Youth transitions must therefore be viewed from the standpoint of both the choice patterns of young people and the ways in which economic and social policies help to shape opportunities.

One should avoid facile comparisons between the experiences of young homeless people and the experiences of others who may appear more fortunate. The combination of circumstances that lead an individual to become homeless may often include a large element of chance, and it is vital that we seek to foster a sense of inclusion rather than exclusion if we are to help young people to progress towards full independence. Hence, young people who are homeless may be amongst the most disadvantaged in our society by virtue of their homelessness but may not necessarily have been so before they became homeless.

The role of the family in homelessness

There are as many different pathways into homelessness as there are homeless people, so generalisations are fraught with danger for good practice. Family difficulties of various kinds do undoubtedly play a major part, in many cases, and it is not uncommon, when young people are asked why they became homeless, to hear reasons like:

> Through family dispute. If ye want ye can add in violence as well. (Young woman aged 20)

> I fighted with my father because he was fighting with my mother. (Young man aged 18)

In Glasgow, 25 young homeless people gave the reasons for their homelessness (see Table 6.1). Some young people gave more than one reason.

Table 6.1 Reasons for homelessness: 25 young homeless people interviewed in Glasgow

Reason for homelessness	Male	Female	Total
Family conflict	10	5	15
Voluntary	1	2	3
Drugs	1	2	3
House repossessed by landlord	1	1	2
Evicted by sibling or partner	1	1	2
Care leaver	0	2	2
Death of parents	1	0	1
Mental health	0	1	1
Violent partner	0	1	1
Not known	1	5	6

Most of these interview subjects declined to give details of problems within their families of origin when given the opportunity to do so, preferring to make an oblique reference to 'conflict within the family', or some similar phrase. A number of different reasons may account for this reticence, which contrasts with the candour with which subjects answered other interview questions. These reasons could include loyalty to the family, embarrassment, and possibly the lack of a comparative perspective. Young people rarely have experience of more than one family and may not be able to assess the quality of the family life that they have experienced.

Friction between the young person, themselves, and one or both parents, or step parents, is also a frequently expressed factor:

> Because I don't get on with my dad, we always have fights but my mum, sister, brother and nephews are all right. Yes! (Young man aged 18)

A wide variety of other reasons are described, however, such as:

> I left my ma's. As I started takin' drugs. I didnae want tae put my ma through all the hassle and shit. (Young woman aged 20)

> My mum asked me to leave because the house is too wee. (Young man aged 16)

Research on homelessness has indicated a startling over-representation of young people who have been 'accommodated'. A study of homelessness conducted by the Department of the Environment found that one in four of those sleeping rough had spent some time in a children's home and one in ten had lived in a foster home (Anderson, Kemp and Quilgars 1993). These are very conservative figures, with much higher percentages suggested by other studies.

Few if any of the scenarios portrayed by these brief comments paint a picture of warm and supportive family life. Family dysfunction clearly plays a major part in the circumstances whereby young people become homeless, but this is not the whole story. If it were, then the 'writing off' of the family as a potential positive force in young people's lives might make sense. In fact, in many cases the families in question have experienced significant deprivation, sometimes over generations, prior to the point at which a young person has become homeless. Long-term unemployment, poor housing, overcrowding, low educational attainment and material poverty may all be present. Other families may have suffered a sudden catastrophic series of misfortunes that can transform their situation from one of comfortable routine to a desperate battle for survival, almost overnight. One might conclude that any family's circumstances might change again for the better and that, if they do not, many residual bonds and strengths might remain.

The family as a resource

A revolution in social work thinking about the family took place in the 1960s and early 1970s. Up to that time, residential care was often thought to offer the best possible solution for many children who could not remain at home. Very little family support was available for families experiencing difficulties that we now regard as relatively trivial so the number of children to whom this applied was many times that of children looked after and accommodated today. It is not uncommon to find the view expressed in the files of residential childcare establishments of the 1950s and 1960s that children were 'better off without' their families. This changed radically with the realisation that a child's attachment to parents, and particularly the mother, created the strongest bond that anyone is likely to experience throughout their life and that this bond cannot easily be replaced or replicated. It became generally accepted that family bonds are broken at the peril of the helping agency no matter how flawed or dysfunctional the family might appear to be. This remains the prevailing view amongst social workers practising with children and families.

Similar considerations apply with regard to homeless young people. Despite frequent high levels of family breakdown and conflict, and despite the fact that in some extreme cases it is literally unsafe for young people to live in the family home, family members remain the most important supporters in the battle to achieve independence. We should not be surprised at this fact because it is accepted that family attachments are life-long. Why then, should we expect them to be any less important for young adults than they are for children?

When young people are asked about their preferred sources of help and advice, family members feature prominently, much more so than any professional source of help.

> It depends what kind of problem it is. My friends and family would probably be the ones. (Young woman aged 19)

> Family! Your family's always going to be there for you. It's the one thing you can rely on. (Young man aged 20)

The same 25 young people in Glasgow reported on in Table 6.1 were asked whom they would turn to if they needed help with a problem and their responses are recorded in Table 6.2. Many of the respondents specified more than one potential supporter.

Table 6.2 Preferred sources of help: 25 young homeless people interviewed in Glasgow

Source of help	Subjects responding
Parent	4
Sibling	1
Other family member/family (general)	5
Friend	10
Other (non-professional)	3
Key worker	3
Staff member (other than key worker)	2
Social worker	4
Home maker	1
Specialist addiction worker, etc.	2
Nobody/don't know	6
Total references	**41**

In summary, references to family members of all kinds (10), friends and other non-professional contacts (13), and professionals of all kinds (12) are almost evenly distributed, with six references to being self-reliant, or not knowing who to turn to. These findings seem to indicate that friends and family members as support providers tend to be at least as highly valued as the many professional helpers with whom these young people are in contact. This may be surprising in view of the fractured nature of many of their families of origin.

Continuing family contact

The view that families provide the most important potential support system for homeless young people is not merely a theoretical one. The fact is that the majority of such young people maintain regular high levels of contact with family members, often on an almost daily basis. These include parents (more often separately than together because family breakdown is common), siblings, grandparents, aunts, uncles and cousins. The nature of the contact is often surprisingly ordinary, featuring such routine family activities as sharing meals, watching television, shopping or visiting other relatives. It rarely seems as though the homelessness of a family member is regarded as a continuing crisis causing a great deal of talk and attention. The picture painted by some of the young people's diaries, written during the Quarriers research (see Appendix), seemed to indicate that homelessness was more often a fact that had been accepted and was being worked around with minimal disruption to family functioning.

This even seems to be the case in families where traumatic conflict has occurred in the past. Many who have never experienced homelessness before have noticed a dramatic improvement in relations with their parents once they have left home. There are those who at any given time feel unable to cope with much, if any, contact with their family, but this state is not necessarily permanent, and in any case these young people are very much in the minority.

> Went to my bro's house. Sat in his house hanging put… Played the computer. Went to the internet cafe. Took my little brother and sister to the pictures. (Young man aged 16)

> Had a couple of beers and watched Leeds v Valencia in my sister's. I went to my sister's in [name of district] to watch the football. Sister and nephew and sister's boyfriend. We spoke about life and football. (Young man aged 19)

> Bumped into Dad. Took me to town and got me Fragile by Jean-Paul Gaultier [a perfume]. Cried 'cause it was dear. Dad was talking about how the decorating was going. (Young woman aged 20)

Very few writers about homelessness have considered the ongoing importance or otherwise of family relationships and other social networks until very recently. In the report 'Dreams Deferred', undertaken by Lemos and Durkacz (2002), action research with the homeless service users of a number of London projects is described. The purpose was to map the social networks of these individuals. Among other questions relating to their wider social networks, subjects were asked:

1. Do homeless people still have networks of friends and family, or have they been completely lost?

2. What sort of help could support workers and others provide to assist homeless people in rebuilding old networks of friends and family if they want to, or in establishing new friendships?

Whatever pain had been suffered, the homeless people who took part in the research valued the relationships they maintained and felt the loss of those links that had been broken. They displayed a desire to rebuild at least some of these lost or damaged relationships.

Despite the body of work supporting the view that having a socially dysfunctional family of origin makes a young person significantly more likely to become homeless, comparatively little attention has been paid to the ongoing role of the family in relation to homeless young people. This is surprising in view of the high respect paid by the social work profession to attachment theory, especially in relation to childcare and the continuing importance of the family of origin in situations of substitute family care. Bannister *et al.* (1993), focusing specifically on the role of the social work services in response to youth homelessness, did recommend an expansion of mediation services to maximise the possibility of reuniting young people with their family, where this could be accomplished without exposing them to harm, but such cases are always likely to be in the minority, given the prevalence of abuse and violent family conflict in the backgrounds of many young homeless people.

It seems that the problematic nature of the families of homeless young people has been consistently emphasised rather than their ordinariness. Although many studies agree that family breakdown and other problems within the family home, including 'push' factors such as physical and sexual abuse, are important causes of homelessness amongst young people (Hyde 2006), Hutson and Liddiard (1994) suggest an 'interpretivist' approach, whereby the role and position of any speaker about homelessness must be considered in assessing the value of their words.

This could help to explain why the ongoing importance of family relationships and the frequency of family contacts come as something of a surprise and why families rarely seem to be regarded as a resource for young people who have experienced homelessness. It may be that agencies have found it in their interests to write off families as problematic and of little or no significance when building future support networks rather than engaging with them, through conciliation and mediation services, as ordinary families which have experienced problems but remain ordinary and just as important as any other young person's family.

Risk assessment and the duty of care

Amongst professionals in the social services, the term 'youth at risk' has become commonplace in recent years. The tendency has been described by Bessant (2001) as the 'science of risk':

> It has become part of the contemporary common sense that leaving school 'early', living in certain family arrangements and having a particular socioeconomic or ethnic background put a young person 'at risk' of various other social ills like unemployment, crime, suicide, homelessness, substance abuse and pregnancy. (Bessant 2001, p.3)

The problem with this as a general analysis and guide for practice is that it can lead to a tendency to label young people in defined risk categories. The consequent need for close supervision can delegitimate young people as speakers and 'experts' capable of framing problems in different ways and suggesting new solutions. The families of some young homeless people, although probably a small minority, may in certain circumstances pose a risk to their safety and wellbeing. The social work and social care professions also widely recognise a duty of care whereby a responsibility to intervene in an individual's best interest is accepted where there is danger of significant harm to him- or herself or others. Young homeless people are almost always adults, in the eyes of the law, so the duty of care is a professional rather than a legal responsibility. What is most important, from the practice perspective, is that this responsibility is exercised in a way that does not disempower the young person concerned. Young adults commonly experience frustration when they believe that their freedom of action is being constrained by someone who knows, better than they do, what is in their best interests. When the objective is to help the young person to achieve a sense of confidence in his or her ability to function as an independent adult, it is important that a realistic appreciation of risk is owned and understood by the young person.

'Person Centred Planning' is a set of tools and techniques that places the recipient of support at the centre of the helping process. Although it is more often used in services for disabled people, it is equally applicable in other settings, including services for the homeless. A seven-step risk assessment is often used, *with* rather than *for* the individual being supported, in order to gain a realistic appreciation of risk in any given situation and to determine how that risk should be addressed. Such an approach may sometimes need to be used in relation to a young person's contact with his or her family of origin. In brief, the seven steps are as follows:

1. Identify the activity which the person wishes to undertake.

2. Identify the goals for the person relating to the activity.

3. Identify what the benefits are and who will benefit.

4. Identify the risks and who might be at risk. Record what is already in place to prevent the harm from occurring and the current level of risk.

5. Decide what further action(s) needs to be taken to achieve goals and minimise risk.

6. Record the level of risk following planned actions. Decide if the risk is acceptable and how urgently any actions from the risk assessment need to take place. Check to see if the goals have been compromised.

7. Agree timescales for review.

Supporting positive family contact

Risk assessment is also likely to be used in determining whether visitors should be permitted in supported accommodation services for young homeless people. One of the main priorities for any service of this kind should be the need to ensure the safety of both residents and staff (see also Chapter 9). The residents are likely to be vulnerable in a variety of ways as a result of their experiences of life to date and may be at risk of being preyed upon by a range of undesirable elements. However, it is important that visitors are not unnecessarily discouraged, for they have a vital role in the resettlement of the young person. Young people are keenly aware of the stigma attached to being homeless and are very likely to feel ashamed of living in a 'hostel'. This creates one of the main barriers to the maintenance and rebuilding of social networks (see also Chapter 7).

It is particularly helpful if these feelings of shame and isolation can be overcome to the extent of facilitating a visit to the young person's new temporary home by family members, particularly in the first few days after his or her arrival. This is common practice in other areas of life, such as university entrance, or starting at a new boarding school, but is comparatively rare in establishments for young homeless people for the reasons outlined above. A new environment, once visited and experienced directly, however, loses much of its ability to engender fear and foreboding. The young person becomes less preoccupied with shame about his or her situation and the family accept the new reality and adjust to it more quickly. Ongoing family contact immediately becomes more likely.

How then can the worker help the young person to overcome the strong negative feeling, which may exist on both sides, so that this can happen? There is, of course, no infallible formula but the counselling role of workers in these services, which is such an important part of their task, comes into play. If the worker has the time, space and skills to allow young people and family members to talk at their own pace about areas that concern them, then even difficult areas can be talked about. As we have already seen, there are likely to be few, if any, more difficult areas than the things that have gone wrong within the family. It is important to remember, however, that these negatives are, at least partly, counterbalanced by positive recollections in almost every family. What family is totally devoid of hopeful and happy memories and dreams, particularly around the birth of the child who has now grown into the homeless young person? Once the mixture of anger, joy, hope and despair that surrounds these events can begin to be expressed, even obliquely, then the possibility of positive contact becomes a reality.

I am not suggesting the workers in services for the young homeless become psychotherapists but that their role in talking to people is vital for the success of the service. Many of the skills required for this work can be learned, but some cannot. In selecting staff for these jobs, importance should be attached to their 'emotional intelligence' or at least their potential to acquire it. This term refers to the ability to recognise one's own feelings and those of others and to manage emotions both in self and within relationships (Goleman 1998). We will return to the question of the skills and qualities needed by staff in Chapter 10.

Helping young people to cope with family failings

A good deal of the previous section also applies here. Because family dysfunction features in the backgrounds of many homeless young people, there will almost inevitably continue to be times when families let them down, at least in their eyes. This may provoke feelings of anger and resentment and staff may often be on the receiving end of emotional outbursts. Other young people may appear hardened to the impact of such feelings, but may simply be internalising them. There is little if anything that staff can do to 'soften the blow', although they may feel a burning desire to do so, especially if they have worked closely with the young person for some time and a bond has developed. The most important thing is to avoid inadvertently reinforcing negative feelings by agreeing with them, in a well-meaning attempt to empathise. On hearing the latest catalogue of family failings, the worker should never, in effect, be heard by the young person to be saying, 'How awful for you to have such a terrible family'.

Anger and self-pity are not difficult or particularly positive emotions for any of us to summon at such times. Much more helpfully, the worker can try to challenge these feelings and introduce an element of empathy for the family whom, after all, the young person probably still loves. Hence the message received by the young person might be something more like, 'Sure, it's rough for you, but they haven't exactly got it easy, either'.

Having said all of this, it should also be remembered that these matters are intensely private for many young people and that, for much of the time, they may simply not want or be able to talk about them. Their privacy must always be respected, in this regard, but what is most important is that when they are ready to talk, someone with the right understanding is there and ready to listen.

Young people who don't have family support

Some young homeless people will have no live family contacts although, as we have seen, they are likely to be in a very small minority. Only 3 of the 31 young people involved in the Quarriers research in Glasgow had no regular contact with any member of their family. The possible reasons for the complete breakdown of contact are many. Young people who have grown up in substitute care may have lost contact with their family of origin, or in some cases the intensity of the family's problems or geographical displacement may have led to a fracturing of links that cannot easily be repaired. Superficially, it might seem as though these young people can look forward more hopefully to a future unencumbered by family worries and problems but in fact their situation presents them with a significant additional problem.

As human beings grow and develop they learn and acquire the skills needed for survival in a number of different ways. According to Vygotsky (1962) learning can be conscious or unconscious but he particularly identifies the 'zone of proximal development' wherein, using the help of others, the learner gains consciousness and perspective. This comprises all of the things that we learn from working with others and includes many vital survival skills. The 'others' referred to are, more often than not, parents or other family members so an individual lacking all forms of family support has real problems in learning the skills to become an independent adult unless he can find one or more substitutes from whom to learn through prolonged and reasonably intensive engagement.

The substitute(s) does not have to be of the parents' age group or to have any special qualities other than to have some life experience from which he or she has learned in a wide variety of ways. These may be quite commonplace experiences and the nature of the substitute's engagement with the young person can be equally varied and ordinary. One way of achieving this is through befriending and mentoring programmes. A suitably vetted adult volunteer undertakes, through a form of contract, to have regular involvement with a young person over a specified period of time. The maintenance of this commitment by the volunteer is vitally important since the young person's emotional resilience may already have been weakened by his or her past experiences. The commitment involves a choice of activity, jointly arrived at, such as pursuing a shared interest like music or films, or simply meeting for a drink or a meal. Through the regular medium- to long-term contact the young person is afforded the opportunity to gain life skills that they may not otherwise have. Schemes of this kind have recorded high levels of success in helping young people to become independent and high levels of commitment and reward from volunteers.

Of course, befriending and mentoring programmes for young adults may be few and far between. Arrangements of this kind may be difficult to generate without a pre-existing infrastructure. Professionals, whether key workers in specialist services or social workers with case management responsibility, may be tempted to try to take on the substitute role themselves, but I would counsel strongly against it. The professional relationship is potentially affected by too many variables and is not likely to be stable enough to give the young person the security that he or she needs. Even more importantly, it raises the possibility of dangerous confusion between the professional role and that of substitute which, among other difficulties, will make the establishment and maintenance of appropriate boundaries impossible.

Learning points

- Try to avoid the assumption that a young person's homelessness is an indication of his or her extreme vulnerability. To do so is disempowering and, although it may be true of some, most homeless young people are ordinary young people trapped in an extraordinary situation. The routes into homelessness are many and varied but most involve significant elements of chance.

- Don't write off any young person's family, no matter how severe the evidence of family dysfunction may be. It's still the only family he or she has, and family attachments are life-long, even when the family is perceived to have failed any or all of its members.

- Promote positive contact between young people and their families whenever possible. Encourage families to visit young people in hostels and supported accommodation services, especially during the first few days and weeks after their arrival.

- Where there is any suggestion that actual harm to a young person may be implicit within the possibility of family contact a full risk assessment should be carried out. Since these young people are adults, however, the young person should be fully involved and a process such as the 'seven step risk assessment' used that facilitates such involvement.

- Take care to avoid reinforcing young people's negative feelings, especially when they are angry and feel let down by their family.

- Seek appropriate adult befrienders or mentors for young people who lack all forms of family contact. Such an involvement may be important to the young person's acquisition of survival skills.

Conclusion

Theoretical analyses of youth homelessness have tended to blame either the state (structuralist) or the young person and their family (individualist). In fact, neither perspective is particularly helpful in devising the best way to help young people to escape from homelessness and eventually eradicate the problem. In the late 1980s, when youth homelessness began to re-emerge as a significant social problem, the individualist view was paramount and because, for many, the roots of the problem lay in family dysfunction it became common to write off the family as having no further positive use or benefit to the young person. In fact, many young people in this situation continue to receive significant levels of support from their often divided and extended families and without this support would be in even worse difficulties.

For workers in the services tasked with helping young homelessness people, this negative attitude to families is perhaps 'the last taboo'. If we can shed it, whilst still retaining a keen awareness of the harm that some people's families can do to them, then new possibilities are opened up. These young people may have reached the point where they are unlikely to live permanently with their family again, and have reached it a little earlier than the majority of the population. Their family may be far from perfect, but they will always be part of that family and derive support and frustration from it, in varying proportions, as we all do. If we can effectively encourage the positive potential of the family, our ability to help will be greatly enhanced.

References

Anderson, I., Kemp, P. and Quilgars, D. (1993) *Single Homeless People.* London: HMSO.

Bannister, J., Dell, M., Donnison, D., Fitzpatrick, S. and Taylor, R. (1993) *Homeless Young People in Scotland. The Role of the Social Work Services.* Edinburgh: HMSO.

Bessant, J. (2001) 'From sociology of deviance to sociology of risk. Youth homelessness and the problem of empiricism.' *Journal of Criminal Justice 29*, 31–43.

Brannen, J., Dodd, K., Oakley, A. and Storey, P. (1994) *Young People, Health and Family Life.* Buckingham: Open University Press.

Coles, B. (1995) *Youth and Social Policy. Youth Citizenship and Young Careers.* London: UCL Press.

France, A. (1996) 'Youth and citizenship in the 1990s.' *Youth and Policy 53*, 28–54.

Goleman, D. (1998) *Working with Emotional Intelligence.* London: Bloomsbury.

Hutson, S. and Liddiard, M. (1994) *Youth Homelessness: The Construction of a Social Reality.* Basingstoke: Macmillan.

Hyde, J. (2006) 'From home to street: Understanding young people's transitions into homelessness.' *Journal of Adolescence 28*, 2, 171–183.

Lemos, G. and Durkacz, S. (2002) *Dreams Deferred: The Families and Friends of Homeless and Vulnerable People.* London: Lemos and Crane.

Vygotsky, L.S. (1962) *Thought and Language.* Cambridge, MA: MIT Press.

7

Friends and Acquaintances

Helping Young People to Maintain and Rebuild Social Networks

Although the existence of informal support networks among homeless people is often referred to anecdotally by workers with the homeless it has not been accorded very much serious attention until recently. Within this informal, anecdotal context it is known that homeless people themselves often place great value on these networks, whilst professionals more often refer to them in a negative context as reinforcers of antisocial and high-risk behaviour. These views have never been adequately tested, however, and the issue of youth homelessness has generally been approached by academics and policy makers alike from either the structural point of view, focusing upon the relationship between the homeless person and state structures, or the individualist point of view, where the emphasis has been on the pathologies of the homeless person and his or her family. Very little attention has been paid to the nature and extent of social interactions between homeless people and others who may or may not be homeless.

Since 2000, the importance of social interaction in homeless people's lives has begun to be recognised. The research underpinning 'Dreams Deferred' (Lemos and Durkacz 2002) with homeless people in London showed that friendships, as well as family contact, were vitally important to homeless people. They not only required the kinds of support defined in the criteria of Housing Benefit and Supporting People, such as budgeting and household maintenance, but also help with building and maintaining the sorts of relationships that are essential to a happy and fulfilling life. This chapter will examine the nature of social functioning amongst young adults and consider how different aspects of the condition of homelessness make it more or less difficult to form friendships. Finally we will try to identify practical strategies aimed at encouraging positive social interaction and their importance in the task of helping young people to develop into independent adults capable of fulfilling their own aspirations.

Cliques, crowds and gangs: Typical patterns of adolescent relationships

Cotterell (1996) comments that relations with others lie at the heart of the adolescent experience. Young people are concerned with making and keeping friends and they expend a great deal of effort in order to do so. For this reason, if for no other, examination of peer group relationships is vitally important, and the fundamental question must be how the experience of homelessness and life in a hostel or supported living environment affects something so central to young people's lives.

The term 'peer group' has been used in a number of different ways. A distinction may be drawn between three broad types of adolescent peer group – cliques, crowds and gangs – all of which are based upon face-to-face interaction (Cotterell 1996). Cliques are natural groupings of peers, whilst the term 'crowds' has been used to describe larger groupings, where several cliques have amalgamated (Dunphy 1969). Gangs, which are less relevant here but about which there is an extensive literature, are tightly knit social groups, often associated with criminal or deviant behaviour and/or control over a location or neighbourhood.

It is also common, however, for the term 'peer group' to be used in a more general sense, referring not to young people who interact directly in a group but those with whom a person may identify in some way. These may be termed 'reputation-based peer groups' as opposed to 'interaction-based groups', and it is in this more general sense that the term is used here, the common features that may create a sense of shared identity being youth and/or homelessness.

Most young people who become homeless will already have a network of social contacts when they enter the 'service environment' of a hostel or supported accommodation project. These can often be traced back to the school(s) they attended and the neighbourhood(s) where they grew up. Friendships frequently follow a territorial pattern whereby, although they may not be 'gang members' in the accepted meaning of the term, there may be real barriers to social interaction with young people from other neighbourhoods within the same city. Becoming homeless and entering some form of transitional accommodation usually involves young people leaving their home area, since most accommodation for homeless young people is established in city centre locations. When they arrive, they will meet and have the opportunity to make friends with a variety of young people from other districts, whom they would otherwise be unlikely to meet.

The possibility of a common bond developing within this new peer group is very real, due to the dual shared identity arising from the fact that they all share the experience of homelessness and the fact that they are from a broadly similar age group. As we shall see, this peer group identity forms a powerful dynamic which is often central to the experience of homelessness for young people.

The influence of family background on social functioning

Psychological theory would lead us to look for a link between the behaviour and performance of young people in the social arena and their past experiences in life, particularly their early experiences of family life. Attachment theorists, such as Bowlby (1974), conclude that patterns visible within the first 12 months of life resemble those seen much later. In particular, it is suggested that confidence, freedom from fears and anxieties, and expectations of relationships throughout life are largely dictated by the availability of an attachment figure during the earliest years of childhood. Others go much further and the results of one study (Van Vliet-Vissar and Van Ijzendoorn 1987) show that an intensive participation of the father in family life can be compatible with an improvement in the quality of the first-born's attachments. This quality seems to be determined by, amongst other things, the frequency of playful interactions; the frequency of other interactions seems to matter less. Harris and Bifulco (1991) studied a group of women who had lost their mother before they reached the age of 11. They found that depression was more prevalent in this group than amongst those with no loss of mother. They also found that in one-quarter of those more vulnerable women, inability to make friends was a distinguishing feature.

It is widely accepted that children who either lack secure attachments or suffer disturbed early relationships continue to experience relationship difficulties through adult life. The high prevalence of family breakdown in the backgrounds of many young homeless people might make it safe to assume that these young people were predisposed to loneliness and difficulties in forming satisfactory relationships. The limited research findings in this area suggest that there is no such simple causal relationship.

The Quarriers research (see Appendix) followed the social interaction of a small group of young people in Glasgow in detail over a short period through the use of diaries. Within the admittedly small sample, there were indeed young people from highly disturbed family backgrounds who demonstrated greatly impaired social skills, but this was not the whole story. Other young people from equally dysfunctional families were popular, outgoing and, in some cases, almost never alone. Others, who appeared to enjoy above-average levels of support from a relatively stable family network appeared to be quite isolated. In fact the findings suggested that an almost infinite variety of family background and social functioning could be discerned with few obvious links.

The differential impact of trauma on individuals at various stages in their childhood and youth makes the picture much more complex. At the same time it is clear that disadvantage does not always weaken the developing personality. Some people become stronger because of it. Perhaps more important and easier to predict is the impact of observable relationship factors upon young people within the homelessness system and on their prospects for successful resettlement.

Stigma and social breakdown

In many cases, it would be desirable if young people were able to maintain friendships arising from their social circle before they became homeless. One of the principal factors that often makes this very difficult is the stigma, real or perceived, attaching to people who are homeless.

My friends come from middle-class backgrounds and I don't want them down in the hostel. For various reasons, such as they don't know that side of life, feel embarrassed and stigmatised: friends from jobs, college, etc. (Young woman aged 21)

Yep! Yvonne, Carol, Stephanie, Nicola. On average I see them about once a month. I don't like them coming near the hostel. It's a pure riddie! [A red face, an embarrassment] (Young woman aged 18, asked whether she kept in touch with friends from her home area and/or schooldays)

There were many similar comments, perhaps partly because homeless people have at times been represented in the mass media in a negatively stereotypical manner to the extent that they have been regarded as 'folk devils' (Cohen 1973). Pickering (2001) describes the phenomenon whereby media involvement in stereotyping helps to generate a 'spiral of significance' that dramatises and escalates the initial cause of concern through the combination and diffusion of 'folk devil' stereotypes. This increases the degree of perceived deviancy and, for those targeted, can inflect it with positive attributes, so that they can find themselves living up to and competing with their stereotypes.

Patrick (1973) offers an example of this process in his vividly described study of 1960s gang culture in Glasgow. He shows how gangs were used as a mechanism by disenfranchised youth to gain a form of status by living up to the stereotypes of themselves, which they avidly read about in newspapers. In this way, they created a reverse of conventional morality, whereby violence and petty crime are perversely reinvented as symbols of power and status. Few examples of such bravado about the condition of homelessness itself can be found, however. Where it does occur, it usually relates to other aspects of young people's lives, which could and do equally apply to young people who are not homeless, such as social activities and patterns of alcohol and drug consumption.

Cullingford (2000) discusses the genesis of stigma in the individual, arguing that perceptions of inequality arise from direct personal experience in childhood and the interpretation placed upon these experiences. Asked why people were homeless, children gave a number of explanations, including personal crisis, the fault of the individual and personal choice. They did not, however, see other people (or themselves) as helpless victims, and Cullingford suggests that children generally have too much of a sense of their own autonomy to accept this notion readily. At the same time, children tended to stress the inexorability of the process: 'once down, people will stay down'.

It is easy to see how these attitudinal patterns, deriving from childhood, influence adult perceptions or, in some cases, persist virtually unchanged into adulthood. For young adults who have themselves experienced homelessness, this can lead to a rather judgemental and pessimistic view of themselves and of other homeless people. As in many other areas of life, low self-esteem is always likely to impair capacity to make and maintain relationships. People who have a poor image of themselves find it difficult to believe that others may find them likeable and, if they don't believe it, the chances are that other people won't believe it either.

> I hate that people look down on ye. (Young man aged 20)

> Homeless people get shat upon… Police, society in general. (Young woman aged 23)

Girlfriends and boyfriends

Another interesting aspect of the Quarriers research in Glasgow was that 8 of the 31 respondents referred in their diaries to a boyfriend, girlfriend or partner during the relevant period, but when interviewed only 4 of the 24 young people admitted to being in a relationship of this kind. In some cases there was a clear discrepancy between the same subject's diary and interview in this regard, even though the time differential was no more than a few weeks.

It is most likely that this points to the transitory nature of relationships of young people whose lives were unsettled. The number of such relationships in this group seems extremely small, given the ages of the young people and the size of the sample. It may be that there is an element of under-reporting, through embarrassment about discussing a very private area of their lives, but it seems more probable that, with regard to both the apparent short duration of such relationships and also their small overall number, the pressures and uncertainties imposed upon young people dealing with the trauma of homelessness militated against the formation of such emotionally demanding relationships.

It seems therefore that at a time when young people are experiencing severe stress and trauma, and are most likely to benefit from secure and lasting relationships, these relationships are placed under such pressure by the situation that they are unlikely to endure. There is very little that workers in services for young homeless people can do about this, other than consistently to adopt practices which reduce stress, promote improved self-esteem and encourage positive social interaction (see below).

The influence of the group

Social identity theorists have advanced the view that group processes and interpersonal processes are fundamentally distinct from one another. They insist that group phenomena must be viewed in their own right. Hence group identity – derived from knowledge of membership of a group, such as residents within a hostel – may, through group images and stereotypes, be more influential than personal history in determining the personal definition of subjects. This may partly explain the often observed fact that many young hostel dwellers seem content to rely on the easy and casual society of fellow residents, rather than more emotionally demanding relationships outwith this immediate group (see below).

A number of writers have described the characteristics of interaction-based peer groups, such as cliques, crowds and gangs. All conform to the accepted understanding of a group as 'a collective of individuals who have relationships to one another that make them interdependent to some degree' (Cartwright and Zander 1968, p.46).

Tajfel (1978) identifies three aspects of group membership:

- Cognitive: the knowledge that one belongs to the group.

- Evaluative: whereby membership is given a positive or negative value.

- Emotional: where cognitive and evaluative aspects are accompanied by emotions such as love or hatred towards one's own group and towards others which stand in certain relations to it.

The creation of a situation whereby young people who have left their home neighbourhood are brought together to live in close proximity under one roof makes the formation of a group bond almost inevitable. There will always be likes and dislikes within the group but, generally

speaking, the members of the resident group are likely to feel an acceptance of one another and a suspicion of outsiders. In this way, the whole
basis of transitional group accommodation for young homeless people
is likely to militate against the maintenance and rebuilding of social
networks in the 'outside' community. This is not to argue against the
existence of such services, or to criticise the way in which they are
operated. There may be little or no practical alternative, if any service is
to be provided at all. It is, however, important to understand the power
of the group and to look for ways to work with it rather than against it.

Groupwork is also a powerful tool in the therapeutic sense. It can
become a crucial intervention when young people have arrived at the
point where they have a real motivation to move out from the comparative comfort of a hostel to an independent tenancy. This step involves
tackling a frightening range of tasks and responsibilities and is a hurdle
at which many fall. If workers can bring such motivated young people
together, in an informal support group, then the power of the support
that such a group can generate for its members will greatly exceed
anything that the efforts of individual workers can achieve. In fact, a
basic familiarity with groupwork theory (Brown 1992) and confidence
in using groupwork techniques in practical everyday settings are among
the essential attributes of effective workers in these settings.

Close and casual friendships

The Quarriers research in Glasgow seemed to indicate that most of its
subjects, all young people living in hostels or supported accommodation projects, tended to have only tenuous, if any, links with friends they
had known before they became homeless. These conclusions must be
treated with caution because of the small sample size and the uneven-
ness of the data, but nevertheless they do provide food for thought.

By reviewing the whole body of data relating to a particular subject,
consisting in most cases of a diary and an interview, and also the context
within which social contacts occurred, it was possible to arrive at a very
crude typology. Four categories were used: casual and close relationships with other residents within the same hostel or project, and casual
and close relationships with others 'outside'. There were, however,
distinct differences between the evidence of friendship patterns
provided by diaries and what those same subjects said about their social
relationships when interviewed. In general terms, most respondents

admitted to considerably fewer friendships in interview than their diaries seemed to indicate. Perhaps many of these relationships were taken for granted or not seen as significant by the subjects themselves.

The peer group relationships referred to in the diaries and interviews are mainly characterised as casual acquaintanceships, friendships and cliques. Friendship, a term that covers all voluntary social relationships, develops in one of the overlapping social worlds that every person inhabits. It might be expected that the captive peer group within a hostel or supported housing project would provide an environment conducive to the formation of friendships, but 20 diaries and 12 interviews referred to social contacts with fellow residents in ways that indicated casual contact.

> I meet up with…my pals outside the hostel every so often, but not as regular as I would like. This is because I have company on my doorstep. (Young woman aged 21)

Only eight diarists and four interviewees indicated that close friendships had developed with other residents perhaps because, as we have already seen, group identity in a 'total living environment' such as a hostel may exert a more powerful influence than it would in a living environment more typical for young people of this age group (i.e. living at home with their parents).

Some of the individuals within this minority may already have been chronically isolated prior to becoming homeless. On the other hand, a few subjects who had indicated a background of serious family problems nevertheless demonstrated an active social life in all areas. A young woman of 18, for example, who had been made homeless as a result of a violent family dispute, said of family contact, 'It can get emotional sometimes and I cannae be bothered wi' it'. Despite having no regular boyfriend, her diary evidenced regular and generally positive contacts with a best friend 'outside', four named individuals from her district of origin and many of her fellow residents. She gave the impression of being a well-adjusted and sociable individual.

The most typical pattern was reversed in relation to outside contacts in that these were more often 'close' than 'casual'. Only 14 diarists and seven interviewees referred to individuals with whom they had contact during the diary period in ways that indicated casual acquaintanceships, whilst 20 diarists and 14 interviewees talked of close friends 'outside' in their diaries and/or interviews. It is concerning – in view of the stated objective of many of the agencies involved in operating these services to find ways of helping young people to become permanently settled – that no more than half of the subjects, at most, had any live social link with people of their own age group in their area of origin. It must be daunting indeed for a person considerably younger in age than the national average for independent living to establish themselves in a new and unknown area. There was little evidence that young people were provided with support and encouragement to maintain and, if necessary, rebuild links with their home area, although it might well have proved a more successful strategy in aiding resettlement.

Promoting positive social activity

Young people leaving the homelessness system with a network of friends and other contacts in the community will stand a far better chance of establishing themselves in their own tenancy than those who do not. It follows, therefore, that it is a vital part of the support worker's role to facilitate the maintenance or development of such a network. If the remnants of such a network remain, then every opportunity should be taken to facilitate the young person's contact with those friends. As with family contacts, however, the proviso must be added that not all friendships are necessarily positive, and in extreme cases it may be necessary to engage the young person in risk-assessing possible harmful consequences.

Many practical barriers may be placed in the path of such contact, not least distance and inaccessibility. The peer researchers involved in the Quarriers research project suggested that the issue of free or discounted travel passes to homeless people would greatly help them to engage in positive social contact. Similarly, in an era when most young people own a mobile phone, talk time may be restricted and the issue of vouchers would help them to keep in touch with friends. It is unlikely, however, that many workers with the homeless would be able to make such provision, so less resource-heavy strategies must be considered.

We have seen that one of the main barriers is stigma. The shame that young homeless people feel at being homeless causes them to withdraw or hide away from the friends who are most able to provide the support that they need. In the constant search for activities to fill a resident's time in a purposeful way (see also Chapter 5), activities that involve only contact with fellow residents or other homeless people, however well-meaning, potentially reinforce this stigma. Wherever possible, mainstream facilities should be used for activity, and workers should utilise the full extent of their ingenuity to find ways of bringing young people into contact with others who are not homeless. For example, community centres and sports centres may be preferable to specialised facilities for the homeless. Participation in a mainstream amateur football league may be preferable to playing matches against teams from other hostels.

It is expected that every young person will have contributed to a plan drawn up with their key worker and other relevant professionals, and in many cases this will identify the area where they eventually hope to be rehoused. This may be their home area, or they may have taken the decision to make a clean break and seek rehousing elsewhere. In either situation, there is an opportunity for the building of local contacts to begin, with the support of staff, as soon as the ultimate preferred destination is determined. It must be acknowledged that housing allocation practices can make it very difficult to be sure where the young person is likely to end up, so early intervention carries the risk of wasted effort. Nevertheless, many workers will have encountered young people completely lost in empty flats, located in areas many miles from any supportive contact. If we are serious about trying to end youth homelessness, we cannot allow this to go on happening.

We have also seen how the easy social environment of the hostel can provide a ready-made alternative to the task of keeping in touch with 'outside' friends, which can be hard work for many young people. Of course, these are adults and there is a fine line between positive influence and unacceptable interference in their lives. Many hostels discourage late-night parties in hostel rooms, however, and also discourage young people from sleeping late in the mornings by providing breakfasts. An active policy of promoting positive activity and social contact, with a programme to which the residents themselves have contributed, will help to reduce the scope for these less helpful patterns to develop.

Isolated individuals

In the literature of agencies working with young homeless people it is common for their personal vulnerability to be emphasised. This may be expressed in terms of disabilities, mental health difficulties, a care background, a family background involving conflict and/or abuse, but is usually accepted as an indicator that high levels of support are needed and that expectations of success should be low. One of the most important findings of the Quarriers research was that although there were some exceptionally vulnerable individuals within the subject group, the majority were striking in relation to their ordinariness and their vulnerability, which could not be separated from their experience of homelessness and the trauma that it often involves. Young people who are homeless typically exhibit a range of personal problems arising from their experiences, both as a homeless person and/or in their earlier lives. In other respects they are broadly similar to any other group of young people of the same age group and from similar social backgrounds.

At the margins of any group of young homeless people there are likely to be a few individuals who show all the signs of being chronically isolated. Young people arriving at a service for the homeless rarely do so with a full 'case history' attached. This is because there is a degree of dislocation between children's services and those for adults. Difficulties and disabilities that may have been fully assessed, and for which intensive support or therapy may have been allocated in the child, may only emerge gradually in the young adult. Young people have a choice about how much of their past life and experiences they reveal to others, including workers in services for the homeless. This may sometimes mean that, in the absence of any clear and unequivocal explanation from the young person themselves, it will be impossible to make a firm judgement about the cause of these characteristics.

One of the greatest and most frequently expressed frustrations of workers in these services is the difficulty of providing effective help for the minority of residents who remain chronically isolated and therefore largely immune to most of the practical strategies available to support them. Workers may suspect that a learning disability or mental health problem is at the root of the problem. Such individuals sometimes become 'stuck' in a service because, although it may not be the right place for them, it can be very difficult to move them on to an environment where support more effectively geared to their particular needs is available, even if such an alternative exists. It is very easy to advise that referral on to more specialist forms of assistance is the right approach for isolated individuals, but the difficulty of accessing such services cannot be underestimated. Furthermore, the agreement of the young person is an essential prerequisite of any such referral and that may not be forthcoming, either because he or she is reluctant to appear 'different' in any way, or because he or she may have had negative experiences of such services during childhood.

Gender differences

Friendship patterns may differ according to gender. Feminist writers (Griffiths 1995; Hey 1997) suggest that girls' friendships tend to be deeper and longer lasting than those formed between boys because of girls' different experiences, including restrictions about where and when they could go out. They conclude that the strength of their relationships enables girls to compensate for these restrictions to some extent by asserting some measure of power and control. Williams and Giles (1978) assert that females are, because of their dependence on the 'out group', unlikely to resort to violent or extreme social behaviour to attain their goals, and this may also, in effect, remove a barrier to the formation of friendship that exists amongst males. The results of a major study undertaken by a team from Manchester University announced in 2007 (Tampubolon and Savage 2007) found the quality of friendships differed considerably between the sexes. The findings suggested that men tended to form friendships as a byproduct of leisure activity, such as someone with whom they could go to football matches or play golf. Women, on the other hand, it was claimed, defined themselves by their friendships which they valued for their own sake and put more effort into keeping alive.

The gender split of the subject group in the Quarriers research was almost even (16 females and 15 males). The feminist position was supported by the finding that six female subjects, but only two of the male subjects, indicated in their research diaries that they had formed close friendships with fellow residents. When asked directly about this in interview, only two females and two males admitted to close friendships with fellow residents. When subjects were asked about close relationships outwith the immediate residential environment, however, the difference between the responses of male and female subjects was less extreme. In their diaries, 12 females and eight males referred to such relationships, whilst in interview, the split was six females and seven males, respectively.

It may be that female respondents were generally more sociable but placed less importance or value upon acquaintanceship, as opposed to friendship, because the males made greater reference to casual relationships, especially within the project. Whilst one might hesitate to draw firm conclusions from such a small sample, it seems clear on the basis of these data that females were generally more interested and active in the area of close friendship than males, to whom such a concept seemed less relevant. On this basis, it may be easier and more straightforward to support young women who are homeless in the task of maintaining and rebuilding social networks than it is to support young men in the same situation but, of course, reality is rarely that simple and the situation is likely to be clouded by many other interposing factors.

Learning points

- Don't assume that the background of any young person necessarily determines his or her social skills, or lack of them. Things are rarely that simple.

- Stigma and low self-esteem form powerful barriers to positive social activity. Any promotional strategy should be tested on the basis of its potential to challenge these barriers.

- The trauma implicit in the experience of homelessness places heavy pressure on all relationships.

- Group bonds develop between young people living under the same roof. Groupwork can be a powerful tool in the hands of the skilled worker.

- Whilst relationships between fellow residents tend to be characterised as 'casual acquaintanceships', terms like 'close friends' are more often reserved for those known before the individual became homeless.

- Being unable to afford public transport or telephone calls can impair social functioning.

- The use of mainstream community facilities for activities which involve contact with people who are not homeless can help to reduce stigma.

- A minority of chronically isolated individuals will inevitably present severe challenges to services. Specialist help may be needed but can only be accessed with the full agreement and participation of the young person.

- A developing 'party scene' within projects may sometimes need to be subtly discouraged.

- Gender differences in friendship patterns should be taken into account. Generally speaking, young women seem to be more highly motivated to make and maintain close friendships than young men.

Conclusion

Although the strength of early attachments and the power of the group are both relevant factors in the social functioning of young people, social network theory is perhaps more relevant than either in helping us to understand the way in which young people derive support from others. As well as mapping social contacts, the significance of the social network also helps us to appreciate the quality of the relationships themselves. It is those ties with others in the network, which subjects describe as 'strong' (i.e. close rather than casual contacts), which involve greater emotional intensity and potential influence. Hence young people who have strong ties to a network of friends and other contacts, outwith their immediate living environment, are most likely to find the support necessary to establish themselves successfully as independent adults.

The development of a young person's social network and the support needed to achieve it must be considered a high priority for services and not, as has so often been the case in the past, at best an irrelevance and at worst something to be discouraged.

References

Bowlby, J. (1974) *Attachment and Loss: Separation, Anxiety and Anger (Volume 2)*. New York: Basic Books.

Brown, A. (1992) *Groupwork, third edition*. Aldershot: Ashgate.

Cartwright, D. and Zander, A. (eds) (1968) *Group Dynamics: Research and Theory*. London: Tavistock.

Cohen, S. (1973) *Folk Devils and Moral Panics*. St Albans: Paladin.

Cotterell, J. (1996) *Social Networks and Social Influences in Adolescence*. London: Routledge.

Cullingford, C. (2000) *Prejudice: From Individual Identity to Nationalism in Young People*. London: Kogan Page.

Dunphy, D.C. (1969) *Cliques, Crowds and Gangs*. Melbourne: Cheshire.

Griffiths, V. (1995) *Adolescent Girls and Their Friends: A Feminist Ethnography*. Aldershot: Avebury.

Harris, T. and Bifulco, A. (1991) 'Loss of parent in childhood, attachment style, and depression in adulthood.' In C. Murray Parkes, J. Stevenson-Hinde and P. Marris (eds) *Attachment Across the Life Cycle.* London: Routledge.

Hey, H. (1997) *The Company She Keeps: An Ethnography of Girls' Friendship.* Buckingham: Open University Press.

Lemos, G. and Durkacz, S. (2002) *Dreams Deferred: The Families and Friends of Homeless and Vulnerable People.* London: Lemos and Crane.

Patrick, J. (1973) *A Glasgow Gang Observed.* London: Methuen.

Pickering, M. (2001) *Stereotyping: The Politics of Representation.* York: Palgrave.

Tajfel, H. (1978) 'Interindividual behaviour and intergroup behaviour.' In H. Tajfel (ed.) *Differentiation Between Social Groups.* London: Academic Press.

Tampubolon, G. and Savage, M. (2007) *The Social Structuring of Closest Friendships: A Creative Assembly.* Manchester: University of Manchester, Centre for Research on Socio-Cultural Change. Unpublished.

Van Vliet-Vissar, S. and Van Ijzendoorn, M.H. (1987) 'Attachment and the birth of a sibling: An ethnographic approach.' In L.W.C. Tavecchio and M.H. Van Ijzendoorn (eds) *Attachment in Social Networks.* Contributions to the Bowlby-Ainsworth attachment theory. Amsterdam: Elsevier.

Williams, J. and Giles, H. (1978) 'The changing status of women in society: An intergroup perspective.' In H. Tajfel (ed.) *Differentiation between Social Groups.* London: Academic Press.

8

Drugs and Alcohol

Dealing with Substance Misuse

This is not primarily a book about substance misuse or addiction issues, about which there is already a voluminous literature. No attempt will be made therefore to offer new or definitive approaches to these perennial problems. Since drugs and alcohol, though, have such a high profile in services for young homeless people, a book of this kind would be incomplete without an attempt to find an appropriate perspective on substance misuse in homeless young people. Managers and workers in these services have often stated over many years that drugs, in particular, have completely changed their task and made it much more difficult. It seems that the supply and use of drugs of all kinds has an insidious quality and has the ability to infiltrate any location accessible to young people.

At the same time alcohol, arguably one of the most harmful of all drugs, but legally supplied and barely controlled, is ubiquitous. The general public and the mass media frequently assume that excessive drinking and drug taking are linked with homelessness. It is therefore important to consider whether there is such a link and, if so, what is its nature? Then we shall examine the practical implications of substance misuse for services and consider what can be done to provide the best possible assistance for those with addiction problems who are also looking for help. Finally we shall address how a positive culture with regard to substance misuse can be generated within a service and how it can be kept in the ascendancy, when threatened by other more seductive cultures.

Why do young people take drugs and drink to excess?

The extensive literature on addiction contains numerous explanations for a phenomenon that has preoccupied so many since the early 1970s. No fewer than nine different strands of theory have been recorded (Neale 2002) and these are generally equally applicable to drug use and problem drinking. It is important to develop an individual standpoint on these issues, which will then inform practice, but this is not a theoretical textbook and, in order to achieve this, it is necessary to simplify the picture greatly. In fact, Neale's nine strands can be separated into two dominant theoretical trends: 'individualist' and 'structuralist'.

Individualistic explanations have highlighted the possibility that drug users may suffer from some form of illness or deficiency, including pre-existing and possibly inherited physiological or metabolic deficiencies. In recent years, individualist explanations have also drawn on post-modernist ideas and linked with underclass theories in emphasising the importance of family breakdown and individual choice as causes of deviance (Jones 1997). Becker (1963), and others who followed him, developed the notion of 'careers' that applied to substance abuse, as well as other forms of deviancy. They abandoned the notion that users suffer from some form of underlying psychopathology and instead emphasised the element of rational choice, whereby drug users adopted a lifestyle, which happened to be deviant, and passed through a number of career stages, just as others do in non-deviant careers.

These theories that look to the characteristics and circumstances of the individual for explanations are challenged by a range of structural approaches that all pose a direct link between structural problems in society, such as poor housing, unemployment and deviancy, including drug use and problem drinking. Where individuals find that their path towards conventional goals is blocked, they may reject both the goals and the channels to obtain them. These are likely to be goals that society recognises, such as a good job or a nice house. Individuals in this situation, it is argued, are likely to resort to various forms of deviancy, including drug use. These theorists believe that it is necessary to break into the wider circle of deprivation, in order to tackle the problem of drug use effectively.

In fact, neither individual nor structural explanations are totally sat-isfactory to the author, especially when the views of young people are taken into account. The Quarriers research in Glasgow (see Appendix) found evidence that many of the young people participating had expe-rienced situations of personal and social deprivation that may have reduced their real or apparent opportunities for advancement and fulfil-ment. They also demonstrated, and in some cases articulated, a level of personal choice and independence that does not fit with the classic structural analysis. These young people would have been horrified to learn that others viewed their drug taking and drinking as behaviours driven by structural forces that they could not control. Most young homeless people, if asked, make it quite clear that, if they take drugs or drink to excess, they do so because they want to.

It seems that drugs assume a greater importance for marginalised and disadvantaged young people than they do in 'mainstream youth culture'. Melrose (2000) suggests some examples of the many possible functions that drugs may fulfil for these young people, including a means to reject adult society from which these young people already feel excluded, a way of feeling 'ordinary' by participating in activities that appear to be regarded as normal by their less vulnerable peers, or a means of escape from the routine pressures of a stressful life. It is so diffi-cult to disentangle the motivations which lead individuals to take drugs that it is perhaps pertinent to quote William Burrough's observation: 'You become a narcotics addict because you do not have strong motiva-tions in any other direction' (Burroughs 1977, p.15).

The prevalence of drug and alcohol abuse

For the present purpose, 'drugs' may be defined as those non-prescribed substances the consumption of which, by young people, has been recorded. These change considerably over time since consumption patterns are inevitably driven by market factors such as availability and price. At the time of the Quarriers research in Glasgow, the available drugs were cannabis, heroin, methadone, amphetamine, valium, pain killers (unspecified) and ecstasy. This inevitably rules out a number of substances which might justify consideration, but which were not men-tioned or regarded as drugs by the subjects, tobacco being an example.

Although clearly a drug under a broad definition, and one which is almost universally consumed by young people who are homeless, it is rarely mentioned in the research literature in the context of drug taking. Hence it is ruled out of further consideration here. 'Alcohol' may be defined as any alcoholic beverage mentioned by the subject group in a context of consumption

Evidence points to a significant level of consumption of drugs and alcohol in every part of British society. We are concerned here specifically with young people, and there is plenty of evidence that drug taking and heavy drinking are prevalent amongst young people.

> In summary then, despite the different research methods and patchy geographical coverage, we can piece together a useful overview. Drugs availability and drug trying has increased rapidly, especially amongst young people, and compared with levels described in the 1980s, the rise is phenomenal. Drug trying now begins at around 12–14 years and incidence and prevalence increase with age into the early twenties. The range of lifetime prevalence (i.e. ever tried) is between 25 per cent and 50 per cent by the age of 20. (Parker, Aldridge and Measham 1998, p.15)

It has been estimated that between one-half and one-third of all young people have tried an illicit drug by the time they are 15. Another recent study found that half of the young people sampled had first used an illicit drug between the ages of 12 and 14 and that one-quarter had first tried drugs before they were 12. Three-quarters had therefore tried an illicit drug before they were 14 (Melrose 2000). Patterns of consumption may have changed markedly over time, but virtually all studies are agreed that, from the mid-1960s up to the present, drug use and alcohol consumption have been commonplace activities by the young and have been recognised throughout that period as significant social problems.

A culture of heavy alcohol consumption by young people is even more commonplace than drug taking, especially in the West of Scotland. Alcohol consumption may be more socially accepted than drug taking, but it is commonly regarded as equally harmful by those charged with the support and rehabilitation of these young people. Surveys amongst young people have consistently found that the proportion who had never tasted alcohol was below 10 per cent, but that 13 to 16 per cent of 16-year-olds could be described as heavy drinkers (Fossey 1994). Plant and Foster (1991) found that the overall proportion of heavy drinkers was greater for Scottish teenagers than for their English counterparts.

Melrose (2000) found that both licit and illicit substances were widely available in the areas where the subjects of her study had grown up and that the law appeared to present no barrier to obtaining them. Both her study and others of recent years (Neale 2002) have focused on the use of opiates, especially heroin and methadone, as these have become commonplace throughout society. This change appears to be largely a consequence of increased availability, and Neale found that: 'Heroin was commonly available within a few doors of most people's homes and was particularly accessible in town centres and amongst street homeless and hostel populations' (Neale 2002, p.70).

Plant (1975) and others found that in the past substance abuse was a primarily male phenomenon. Melrose (2000) reported findings that support the view that the situation has reversed since the mid-1970s and that many 'hard drug' users are now women.

Chicken or egg? Why is substance use such a problem for services for the young homeless?

Although attitudes to drug taking and drinking amongst homeless young people seem fairly typical for their age group, there is widespread agreement that actual drug and alcohol use is more prevalent amongst vulnerable groups than in the general population of young people of a similar age (Goulden and Sondhi 2001). These groups include the homeless and runaways, as well as school truants and excludees, young offenders and young people living in drug-using families. What is less certain, however, is the nature of any causal link. It could be argued that a predisposition to substance abuse is yet another manifestation of these young people's vulnerability. On the other hand, it is much more likely that access to drugs, for example, is easier for members of these vulnerable groups and that the stresses of disaffection provide an increased motivation.

The attitude towards drugs and alcohol displayed by young people involved in the Quarriers research seemed typical of young people generally. It is widely believed in professional circles, however, that the prevalence of drug taking amongst young homeless people, together with the criminal subculture that accompanies it, has become a major factor to be addressed if services designed to meet the needs of such young people are to be successful. There is, however, disagreement about the scale of the problem in relation to homeless young people. The use of 'hard' drugs amongst young people who have ever slept rough has been found to be as much as four to ten times higher than amongst young people who have never been homeless, whilst even the non-rough-sleeping homeless used 50 per cent more cannabis (Goulden and Sondhi 2001). Another source (Wade and Barnett 1999) estimates that around 70 per cent of all homeless people are drug-dependent, whilst Bruce (1999) suggests a prevalence of only 30 per cent drug misuse amongst the homeless population. These widely differing estimates may be the result of the pressures towards under-reporting but should also be treated with some caution because of the methodological difficulties involved in gathering the data.

There are as many different modes of substance use as there are substances and, as we shall see below, several distinct patterns can be discerned amongst hostel populations. One tentative conclusion that might be drawn from a number of studies is that the use of opiates (heroin and methadone) is more likely to be linked with vulnerability than other modes of drug/alcohol use. The issue of vulnerability is by no means a simple one, however. The sample participating in the study described by Melrose (2000) was a multidisadvantaged group. Generally speaking, Melrose's subjects themselves could see no direct link between their experience of homelessness and the various indicators of vulnerability, many of which applied to them. She also found, however, that the link was a complex one and not a case of straightforward cause and effect. Viewed in the context of a timeline applying to each individual subject, drug use sometimes came before other vulnerability factors, sometimes after, or sometimes contemporaneously. Around 50 per cent of her sample started using drugs after becoming vulnerable through offending, school exclusion and/or being looked after. A recent study of homeless youth in Australia (Martijn and Sharpe 2006) found that whilst the rates of psychological disorders at the point of homelessness were greater than in normative samples, the rates of clinical disorder increased once homeless.

The distinction between 'drug-driven' and 'drug-related' behaviour has also been highlighted by Neale (2002), who asked 59 homeless people the reason for their most recent episode of homelessness. Drug use was the reason given by 13 subjects, equalling relationship breakdown as the most common cause. On the other hand, Neale (2002) also describes some individuals who revealed that homelessness was a reason why they started to use illicit drugs and highlights the deleterious effect which heroin use has on people who are already homeless. She quotes the widely held view that it is virtually impossible to 'get off' heroin if one is homeless, due to stress levels and/or availability.

Secrecy and criminality

One of the main reasons why drug use is regarded as such a big problem for services for young homeless people is the climate of secrecy that surrounds it. Young people will sometimes and in certain circumstances go to great lengths to conceal their drug use. This is inevitable, since the use of these substances is, by definition, criminal, but a more immediately relevant dimension of secrecy is explained by the difficult position of agencies providing services.

As part of the Quarriers research project, agencies were asked whether addiction and/or social use of drugs were day-to-day issues for the agency and what was the agency's policy in this regard. Five agencies, who were all major providers of supported accommodation for homeless young people, said that although, 'significant numbers have hard drug addiction or alcohol dependency', a strict policy of non-use within the service was in place. The following comment was fairly typical, in this regard:

> Officially, no illegal drugs, alcohol or solvents are allowed to be brought into the project. Residents found with these items, distributing them to others, or being found under the influence can be immediately evicted.

The legal position means that it would be dangerously irresponsible for agencies to adopt any other attitude but the use of the word 'officially' may indicate a degree of covert acknowledgement that these substances are in fact very widely used within these services. Four of these agencies indicated that they did, on occasion, accommodate young people on prescribed medication, including methadone. One agency said that, with regard to addiction:

> The unit is not drug/alcohol rehab, but no substances are allowed on the premises. We have access to a methadone programme and accommodate people who wish to address their addiction.

The same agency's response to the question on social use was forthright: 'No – no social use'.

The other three agencies prepared to accommodate young people on methadone prescription outlined a more flexible policy. One stated:

> Yes, we do not accommodate active users of any substance. However, people in recovery can be supported. Always potential for 'topping up' or drinking. External agencies are involved to provide support to individual tenants as required. If persistent or unsafe issues arise, the placement may as a last option be withdrawn.

Another of these three agencies expressed a broadly similar policy, somewhat differently:

> We aim to work with young people and support them in their attempts to reduce, maintain or cease their drug use. We challenge illegal drug use and have set procedures for dealing with this issue within the project.

With regard to social use, the same agency responded:

> Young people are not permitted to drink or take drugs within the project. Social use is promoted, if this is chosen by service users as 'normal' social activity. If this is problematic, then a plan of action is agreed, to combat this.

It is understandable, in view of the foregoing, that residents of transitional accommodation services are often reluctant to be open about their substance use, since to do so might lead to their summary eviction and a return to the streets. Within this climate of secrecy and criminality, substance use and dealing can easily take hold, and this tendency, or the fear of it, partly explains the concern of almost all professionals in this field about these issues. The possibility that a vulnerable, but non-drug-using, young person might be sucked into a covert drugs scene within a service for young homeless people is obviously a scenario that must be viewed with concern, if not alarm.

> There are people who are dealing (staff don't know), getting people involved in the drug scene (Young woman aged 21).

Risk and resiliency

Workers with young homeless people will inevitably seek to examine the prevalence of various 'risk' and 'resiliency' factors within both individual young people and the overall population of a hostel or project and seek to determine whether any predisposition to problematic substance use can be discerned. Perhaps the most widely accepted indicators of vulnerability are:

- negative or few experiences of family life

- a history of offending behaviour

- negative experiences of education and/or exclusion from school

- being, or having been, looked after.

Many of these factors have been found to be readily evident amongst young homeless people and might be thought to predispose the individual to drug use or problem drinking. An analysis of the vulnerability of any such group can, at best, be tentative because the information provided by them is likely to be incomplete. In one sense, all are vulnerable, because they have experienced, or are experiencing, homelessness. In another sense, many are vulnerable on account of their age, which is generally below the average for home-leavers in this country (see Chapter 6). Few, if any, will be in full-time paid employment and, in this respect, mirror Neale's (2002) study, in that those of her subjects who had worked had mainly been in casual low-paid jobs. In this context, she wrote: 'In the competitive world of job-seeking, drug users did not seem well-placed' (Neale 2002, p.95).

In relation to the four factors outlined above, however, some broad indications emerge. The tentative conclusion that might be drawn from a number of studies, including the Quarriers research, is that opiate use is more likely to be linked with vulnerability than other modes of drug/alcohol use. On the other hand, resiliency skills have also been identified (Melrose 2000), including an easy temperament, intellectual capabilities, self-efficacy, empathy and humour, and many of these skills will also be readily apparent within any group of young homeless people. Workers should seek to identify and encourage such positive characteristics in order to maximise the individual's ability to overcome his or her problems, rather than be overcome by them. The Health Advisory Service (1996) has identified as important in developing resilience to drug-related problems a caring relationship with at least one adult and external systems of support that encourage positive values. This may provide another indicator of the positive value of befriending and mentoring schemes for young homeless people (see also Chapter 6).

Opiate addiction

Two subjects of the Quarriers research (one male and one female) revealed that they were using heroin during the two-week period over which they kept a diary. Hence, a young man aged 20 wrote in his diary: 'Went into the town. I bought a bag of kit and smoked it then came home and watched TV'.

It would appear that in both cases the drug was being smoked, rather than injected, and this was done clandestinely. A female hostel resident aged 20 wrote:

> This morning I went to the doctors with B. She stays in [name of hostel] and is waiting to be put on a methadone script. After the doctors we went to the [name of district] and got a tenner bag of kit, and smoked it on the back stairs in the flats.

This mode of usage is not surprising given that heroin use would almost certainly have precluded the individual's admission to the hostels in question, if known about in advance, or led to their eviction if discovered later. It does not, however, provide any reliable evidence about the nature or severity of the dependency experienced by the subjects in question. Other studies have found that many users progressed from smoking to injecting for purely utilitarian reasons. Injecting is often considered a less wasteful and more cost-effective method of self-administration (Neale 2002). Some services do, however, accept young heroin users who were being prescribed methadone, a synthetic heroin substitute, as part of their rehabilitation programme. Another five young people (two male and three female) involved in the Quarriers research came into this category and this did not include either of the two who described buying and smoking heroin in their diaries.

Methadone is normally prescribed via a specialist drug treatment clinic by a doctor with experience in the treatment of drug dependency. Users are normally allocated to a drug counsellor and would therefore tend to visit the clinic on a fairly frequent basis. The methadone itself was administered daily in the form of a linctus at a designated dispensing pharmacy, normally taken orally and often on the premises in the presence of the pharmacist. The two young people using heroin spent a good deal of their time obtaining supplies of the drug, whilst those on methadone prescription had an almost equally onerous daily routine of visits to the pharmacy, together with slightly less frequent appointments with their doctor and drug counsellor. The extent to which drug taking 'takes over' the lives of users is a moot point, but one can only conclude from the evidence here that opiate addiction was a major, if not dominant, influence on the daily lives of the subjects concerned:

> Later I met another worker for two hours. RG took me to Glasgow Gate, then he took me to the chemist so I could get my 'meth'. Dropped me off. (Young woman aged 20)

> I had to go to [name of district] addiction services and pick up my script. I travelled by bus there and walked back. I met B (doctor) and AM (addiction worker). (Young woman aged 23)

There was a marked difference in the attitude of the subjects who were not taking heroin or methadone to these drugs and other substances, including cannabis and alcohol. The attitude to hard drug users was often judgemental and hostile, typified by statements such as:

> Junkies don't deserve anything, because they're sad individuals. (Young man aged 20)

Cannabis and other drugs

Cannabis is used extensively by young people in Britain, and young homeless people are no exception. It is usually smoked in a 'joint' (a hand-made cigarette containing tobacco and cannabis), in 'bongs' or 'buckets' (crude pipes, often made from plastic soft drinks bottles), 'can pipes', or 'hot knives'. It has often been observed that cannabis smoking is generally a social activity (Plant 1975) and evidence of this tendency was found amongst the subjects of the Quarriers study:

> I got a bit of ganja [cannabis]. I was with the troops. We all had a good smoke sat up late then went to bed. WASTED!!! (Young woman aged 20)

> Me and M got a taxi over to S's. S stays in [name of district], who has been a friend for years, we all sat and listened to music. No one else came up, it was just the three of us, we got stoned and had a laugh and then we got a taxi back home. (Young woman aged 19)

There was also a good deal of evidence of subjects using cannabis on their own as a form of self-medication in order to relax, unwind, or simply for enjoyment. Hence the same 19-year-old young woman, quoted above, also wrote, in another diary entry:

> I made pizza and chips for dinner and had a couple of joints and a couple of can pipes, watched Eastenders...

A 20-year-old female subject wrote in her diary:

> Arrived at dad's had a beer and joint, decided to stay up there as I was very relaxed.

In contrast to the rather censorious attitude often displayed towards opiate use (above), the heavy social use of 'soft' drugs, including cannabis and ecstasy, usually in conjunction with alcohol, is often referred to with a degree of relish and obvious enjoyment:

> Ended up in [name of town]. M, C, T we all got fucking wrecked as far as I can remember. Can't remember a thing. Not got a fucking clue. Fuck knows but I ended up taking an 'E' and smoked a lot of hash then fuck knows what happened after that. (Young woman aged 20)

> ...got booze and smoked hundreds of joints and buckets. STONED HAPPY! IRN BRU BEST FOR BUCKETS! and Went oot n aboot. Out on a mission to brighten the day and it seem as though drugs is the answer. Got blues [valium] and hash. (Young woman aged 19)

The young people involved in the Quarriers research also recorded instances in their diaries of taking drugs other than heroin, methadone and cannabis. These were 'speed' (amphetamine sulphate), 'E' (ecstasy), 'blues' (valium) and pain killers (unspecified). A young man aged 20 recorded that he 'took 30 Blues in C's [a fellow resident's] room'.

No other drugs were specifically mentioned in the course of this research but, as mentioned above, patterns of availability and consumption change due to market factors so, if the same questions were asked today, the list might be different in some respects. Drugs are often taken in combinations, with or without alcohol, in an apparently random manner, according to personal preference and availability. A diary entry by a 19-year-old young woman included the following information:

> Later on I went over to S's with a drink. I took two ecstasy as well and so did S, and then P came up and it was a good night

Whilst another 19-year-old woman included the following entry in her diary:

> Got mad wie it nothing else to do, T got the jail. Everybody loads of hash and scobbie blues.

Whilst these non-opiate drugs are generally regarded as less harmful than opiates like heroin, the legal issues are the same and services cannot therefore condone their use on the premises. In any case there is no clear scientific evidence to support the view that they are harmless. Expert opinion has swung back towards the view that even cannabis can be dangerous when used to excess, especially for those who may have a predisposition to mental health problems. The general acceptability of their use within the adolescent peer group, however, poses a quite different set of problems. Rather than being seen as individuals with problems who need help, as heroin users are often seen by other, non-using, young people, there is a danger that within the superficial social network that develops amongst young homeless people, drug use may come to play such a major part that it significantly distracts young people from addressing their ongoing needs. Prominent amongst these, of course, is the need to escape from homelessness.

Alcohol

Alcohol consumption plays an equal or even greater part in fuelling the 'party scene' that can easily develop in any setting where young people are living in close proximity, including hostels for young homeless people.

It is probably not surprising that 18 of the young people participating in the Quarriers research made specific mention in their diaries of drinking alcohol. In fact, given the prevalence of alcohol consumption by young people in the West of Scotland, it is probably surprising that alcohol did not feature in more of the diaries. Of course, absence of any mention does not mean that alcohol was not consumed. A number of reasons might be suggested for a failure to record, including the commonplace nature of drinking as an activity and a reluctance to admit to something that was against hostel rules (as with drug taking, above).

Ten of those who did record drinking alcohol were female and the other eight were male. There was no discernible pattern as to where and when subjects drank alcohol. On some occasions, they went to pubs and houses:

> Went out for a drink wi people fae hostel came back and went to bed. To pub and to friend's hoose fur a drink. (Young man aged 20)

At other times they drank in a variety of public places:

> Went out for a drink. Up to the park. With C and D two people from my hostel. Talked mostly shite cos we were pissed. (Young woman aged 17)

There was also a good deal of drinking in hostel rooms:

> T and I got a drink. We went to other people's rooms in the hostel. (Young woman aged 21)

It is not possible to deduce from the diaries levels of consumption with any degree of accuracy. Hence, for example, it is impossible to be sure whether those who consumed alcohol could be described as heavy drinkers. A common definition of a heavy drinker would be a male who consumed 50 or more units of alcohol per week, or a female who consumed 35 units or more (Fossey 1994). One, more subjective indicator, however, is frequency with which intoxication was recorded. In their diaries 13 of the 31 young people recorded that at least at one point during their two-week diary period they reached a state of intoxication. Only five of these subjects were male, whilst eight were female, challenging the conventional wisdom that drunkenness/intoxication is primarily a male phenomenon (Plant 1997). It was not possible to determine the exact cause of intoxication in most cases, especially as alcohol and various drugs were often consumed in combinations (see above).

A number of different colloquial expressions were used to denote intoxication, including: 'mad with it', 'pissed', 'stoned', 'out of my nut', 'wrecked', 'out of my face', 'drunk', 'smashed', 'out of my tree', 'wasted' and, in one case, 'maximum entropic state'. Hence, a 19-year-old girl wrote:

> I had a few joints and then went over to S's and got pure wrecked out my face and went home had a munch and went to my bed.

Another young woman, aged 20, recorded an evening during her diary period in the following manner:

> Went and got another drink. Drank hundreds of booze, got pissed. T, M then I met M's pals A, S, wee J and C we all got wasted, brilliant.

A degree of relish can be seen in recording instances of intoxication, but this is not to suggest that the pattern of regular excessive consumption and the habit of equating intoxication with enjoyment were in any way unusual for young people of this age group. Almost all instances of intoxication recorded appeared to be within social situations and, although self-medication features frequently, as described above, the subjects of this study did not admit to getting drunk or stoned on their own. Interestingly enough, only two young people, both male, mention the experience in their diaries of having a hangover which, given the level of consumption recorded (above), must surely represent a degree of under-reporting. A young woman, aged 20, did however write:

> 9.30, head fucking bursting as hangover setting in.

The implications for services of excessive alcohol consumption are much the same as those for 'soft' drug use, except that alcohol is even more widely accepted amongst the relevant social groups and even more readily available. The evidence of its potentially harmful long-term effects are unequivocal and its influence upon behaviour is such that consumption cannot be condoned within services.

Developing a positive culture

Those charged with the responsibility for managing services for young homeless people are severely restricted by legal constraints when it comes to developing a policy for dealing with substance use. It would be grossly irresponsible to pursue a policy that was not fully within the law, and in practice this means that the possession and/or use of any illegal substance, within the jurisdiction of any hostel or project, cannot be condoned. The sympathy of the forces of law and order could not be relied upon in the event of any compromise with this clear principle.

This does not mean that workers are powerless in the face of the apparent universality of drug and alcohol abuse. There is, in fact, a great deal that they can do. Perhaps most importantly, both addiction and social use feed off boredom and inactivity:

> I don't want to sit about smoking all day. I would rather do something that would occupy my time. (Young man aged 20)

In a situation where many young people are effectively excluded from employment, the need for purposeful activity can be acute (see also Chapter 5). Finding a good range of purposeful activities and supporting the sometimes flagging motivation of participants is a constant challenge for workers. Some agencies now regard the provision of such 'alternatives to substance abuse' as so important that they commit significant resources to activity programmes provided in-house or by specialist agencies. Perhaps the simplest definition of a 'positive culture' in such an environment is one where purposeful activity is the norm rather than the exception.

Although some comments by young people themselves about drug and alcohol use have been quoted above, it is likely that few would regard their own consumption pattern as a 'problem' in any way. There are exceptions to this, however, where young people were accepting the help that was on offer and demonstrating some insight into the dangers of their levels of consumption:

> My drink counsellor came up to see me as I have a drink problem. So we sat in my room and had a chat. (Young woman aged 18)

It is vital that those young people who do recognise that they have a potentially serious problem and are prepared to accept help are able to find it, where and when they need it. Successive government policy initiatives about the problem of drug misuse within the UK (Home Office 1998; Scottish Executive 2003) have emphasised the need for integration of addiction services, in the widest sense, in order to make them more effective in achieving the key objectives of reducing substance misuse by vulnerable groups of young people and the harm that it causes. As we have already seen, there is a complex inter-relationship between substance misuse and a range of other vulnerability indicators, including homelessness. There would therefore seem to be a powerful argument for drug and alcohol services to be closely integrated with other services for homeless young people (Wincup, Bayliss and Buckland 2005).

The main thrust of the evidence uncovered by the Quarriers research was that services remain fragmented and compartmentalised, rather than integrated. In 2003, one of the agencies participating in the research project launched an integral addiction service, operating within a supported accommodation project for young homeless people. Early signs of the success of this 'one-door' approach suggest that it may become the template for services addressing these issues.

The need for integration of services extends beyond the 'substance abuse' and 'homelessness' services, however, and takes in many other areas that touch upon the lives of the young people in question. These include education, training and employment (Scottish Executive 2002) and even health promotion, where many believe that young people should be encouraged to address their own substance abuse along with other risk behaviours, that have the potential to influence their life circumstances, such as tobacco smoking and poor diet (Research Unit in Health Behaviour and Change 2004).

Learning points

- Substance abuse is always a matter of personal choice.

- Patterns of drug and alcohol use by homeless young people may not be significantly different from those in the general population of similar age group.

- Addiction feeds off boredom and inactivity.

- There is some evidence that disadvantaged young people, including those who are homeless, may be more likely to misuse substances, but there is real doubt about whether the substance use is a precursor or a consequence of homelessness.

- Services will find it difficult to maintain a full awareness of drug and alcohol use in their environment because it is illegal and/or against the rules and therefore surrounded by secrecy.

- Workers can never implicitly or explicitly appear to be condoning activities that are illegal.

- Risk factors can be minimised and resiliency increased by providing purposeful activities and access to supportive adult relationships such as befriending.

- Opiate addiction has a tendency to dominate an individual's lifestyle and when specialist help is needed and accepted it is most effective if it is integrated, as much as possible, with other services.

- Heavy social use of alcohol and drugs is commonplace and can present a serious distraction to young people as they seek to resolve their problems. A positive culture, which features a good range of alternative activities, is needed to combat this.

Conclusion

The remarkable candour with which the young people involved in the Quarriers research project provided information about their drug and alcohol use, not in response to direct questions but, almost incidentally, through their diaries, has yielded some valuable insights. Opiate use was shown to be, as anticipated, an all-consuming practice with seriously deleterious implications for the user's social functioning and relationships with others. Service providers are right to focus rehabilitative services on this minority of young homeless people, especially where they have the motivation to become 'clean'. What was more unexpected, but equally important, was the extent of what might be called the 'party scene' within hostels and other establishments for the young homeless, involving heavy usage of cannabis, other drugs and alcohol, separately or together in various combinations.

We have established that individual attitudes and practices with regard to usage may not be very different to those prevailing within the wider community of young people of similar age group. Hostels bring groups of young people together to live in close proximity, however, and it is possible that substance abuse in this situation spills over, with the aid of mutual reinforcement, from typical adolescent behaviour to something more serious. It could in some cases, for example, form a real barrier to the very purpose for which these establishments exist: rehabilitation. Further research on this issue is strongly recommended because, if true, it casts serious doubt on the wisdom of providing any services for young homeless people in group living situations.

References

Becker, H. (1963) *Outsiders: Studies in the Sociology of Deviance.* New York: Free Press.
Bruce, M. (1999) 'Co-morbidity.' In C. Stark, B. Kidd and R. Sykes (eds) *Illegal Drug Use in the United Kingdom.* Aldershot: Ashgate.
Burroughs, W. (1977) *Junky.* London: Penguin.

Fossey, E. (1994) *Growing up with Alcohol.* London: Routledge.

Goulden, C. and Sondhi, A. (2001) 'At the margins: drug use by vulnerable young people.' In the *1998/99 Youth Lifestyle Survey.* London: Home Office Research Study, 228.

Health Advisory Service (1996) *Children and Young People, Substance Misuse Services – The Substance of Young Needs.* London: Health Advisory Service.

Home Office (1998) *Tackling Drugs to Build a Better Britain. The Government's Ten-year Strategy for Tackling Drugs Misuse.* Cm 3945. Norwich: Stationery Office.

Jones, G. (1997) 'Youth homelessness and the underclass.' In R. MacDonald (ed.) *Youth, the Underclass and Social Exclusion.* London: Routledge.

Martijn, C. and Sharpe, L. (2006) 'Pathways to youth homelessness.' *Social Science and Medicine 62,* 1, 1–12.

Melrose, M. (2000) *Fixing it? Young People, Drugs and Disadvantage.* Lyme Regis: Russell House.

Neale, J. (2002) *Drug Users in Society.* Basingstoke: Palgrave.

Parker, H., Aldridge, J. and Measham, F. (1998) *Illegal Leisure. The Normalisation of Adolescent Recreational Drug Use.* London: Routledge.

Plant, M. (1997) *Women and Alcohol. Contemporary and Historical Perspectives.* London: Free Association Books.

Plant, M.A. (1975) *Drugtakers in an English Town.* London: Tavistock.

Plant. M.A. and Foster, J. (1991) 'Teenagers and alcohol: Results of a Scottish national survey.' *Drug and Alcohol Dependence 28,* 203–210.

Research Unit in Health Behaviour and Change (2004) *Young People, Cannabis and Family Life.* RUHBC Findings 5. CRFR Research Briefing 14. Edinburgh: Centre for Research on Families and Relationships.

Scottish Executive (2002) *Moving On: Education, Training and Employment for Recovering Drug Users.* Edinburgh: Scottish Executive.

Scottish Executive (2003) *Getting our Priorities Right. Good Practice Guidance for Working with Children and Families Affected by Substance Misuse.* Edinburgh: Scottish Executive.

Wade, G. and Barnett, T. (1999) 'Homelessness, drugs and young people.' In A. Marlow and G. Pearson (eds) *Young People, Drugs and Community Safety.* Lyme Regis: Russell House.

Wincup, E., Bayliss, R. and Buckland, G. (2005) 'Listening to young homeless problem drug users: Considering the implications for drug service provision.' *Journal of Community and Criminal Justice 52,* 1, 39–55.

9

Housing and Support

Working for Sustainable Futures

When studies of youth homelessness have explored definitions of home, young people have been remarkably consistent in their view of what, for them, constitutes the ideal home. They have stressed the importance of security of tenure in a neighbourhood that was 'nice', 'safe' and 'quiet' (Bannister *et al.* 1993; Fitzpatrick 2000). This nearly always meant their own independent tenancy, although Fitzpatrick found that a number of young people (usually male) associated the notion of 'home' with 'family', meaning, in this context, their family of origin. These findings were generally borne out by the Quarriers study (see Appendix), with almost all subjects expressing a desire for their own tenancy.

This chapter describes how services for young homeless people can help young people to achieve these goals. The process of accessing suitable affordable housing is difficult enough but services have the additional duty of providing the support which most young people need, if they are to obtain and keep their own tenancy. In this chapter, we will try to unravel this complex set of tasks and look for evidence about what works best in different circumstances.

Housing supply and demand

In the simplest of terms, there is a shortage of suitable, affordable social housing where young people can be allocated their own tenancy. This shortage contributes to the continuing phenomenon of youth home-lessness and forces many young people to remain within the homeless system for longer than would be the case if the supply more closely matched the demand. Accepting the need for emergency accommoda-tion for those, including young people, who find themselves unexpect-edly homeless, the availability of 'move-on' accommodation, within a reasonably short timescale, is vital. Emergency hostels are inevitably institutional and cannot replicate ordinary daily life. The longer a young person stays there, the more difficulty he or she will experience in adapting to a more independent lifestyle.

During the Quarriers research, a total of 18 agencies working with young homeless people described and/or commented upon processes whereby young people using their services were helped to access suitable move-on accommodation. This represented a reasonably high response rate in the context of the overall response, given that many of the agencies contacted were either providers of non-residential services, or were mainstream housing providers. Seven of the 18 respondents to this question indicated that they found it difficult in some circumstances to access suitable move-on accommodation, or that there was a shortage of such accommodation. Three respondents felt that there was not gen-erally a problem in finding appropriate accommodation options for young people when they were ready to move on. The remaining eight respondents expressed no opinion, but described the processes applica-ble to young people using their services.

Fourteen responding agencies offered opinions about how the 'move-on process' could be improved. Most of these responses fell into one of three categories, which were: more suitable tenancies needed (nine responses); more support required (five) and a wider range of choices in types of accommodation (three). Other responders referred to a perceived need for improved partnership arrangements between providers, a need to speed up the housing allocation process in order to respond to young people's needs at their peak of readiness, and a plea for earlier identification of young people's accommodation and support needs, for similar reasons.

We have already seen how the aspirations of young people in the homeless system tend to be fixed firmly on a home of their own. These aspirations inevitably colour young people's assessment of the hostel or supported accommodation that they currently occupy. Their housing history may also have played a part, since many of them had already spent periods of time in other hostels and some had experienced rough sleeping. Subjects were asked what other types of accommodation they had experienced and one young woman (aged 17) replied: '[name of large general hostel], it's full of junkies and pros and old pervs'. Another young woman (aged 23) offered the following timeline: '[name of hostel] – slept rough – chucked out at 15 – stayed with friends – evicted – rough sleeper – [name of hostel] – rough sleeper'.

Others can reel off long lists of hostels and supported accommodation projects, but some may have already attempted to maintain their own tenancy and lost it, usually through some unforeseen circumstance over which they had no control:

> I had my private rented flat in [name of district] for one and a half years, prior to [name of hostel]. I moved into my own tenancy at the age of 18 years. I became homeless because my landlady fell out with her partner and wanted to move back into her flat. (Young woman aged 21)

The twin strands of aspiration and past experience are often visible in many young people's views of their current situation. Some emphasise the fact that it isn't what they really want. Hence, in response to the questions: 'Where are you living at present? What type of accommodation? How long have you been there? What is your opinion of your present accommodation?' one young woman aged 17 replied:

> [Name of hostel], it's supported accommodation, ten months and it pisses me off. It's alright, but I don't classify it as my home.

Another young woman, aged 21, who had previously twice held her own tenancy and had never before stayed in a hostel, replied to the same questions, as follows: '[Name of hostel]. Hostel. Since the fifth of April – nearly two months. I'm well chuffed. I really, really like it. It's better than I had imagined'. A young man, aged 20, who had listed no fewer than eight hostels for the homeless in which he had resided, responded:

> Here, [name of hostel]. It's a hostel. Seven months. Aye, it's alright.

Subjects were also asked what changes would improve the lot of young homeless people and the same individual replied: 'To stop the system to be so slow. There's too many hooses goan tae the wrong people, like junkies, asylum seekers and that's it'.

The slow speed of housing allocation to young people who had been homeless became a familiar theme in relation to this question, with many young people expressing a degree of frustration:

> There should be better access to housing. You should get your house a lot quicker than you do. (Young man aged 20)

The aspirations of some young people were restrained by circumstances, notably rent arrears, which significantly slowed down the process of escaping from homelessness: 'The Social Work say I cannae get a hoose fur six years 'cause I owe four grand rent arrears' (young man aged 20). It was not possible to establish whether this information was factually accurate, but it was clearly believed by the individual in question.

Another young man, aged 19, voiced the opinion that:

> I would knock every hostel doon and gie everybody a hoose.

Whether he knew it, or not, this comment represented, quite accurately, current housing policy in the City of Glasgow. In 2000, the Glasgow Street Homelessness Review Team reported to the Scottish Executive's Homelessness Task Force and included recommendations that: 'Long-term hostel residents should, wherever possible, be moved into tenancies with appropriate support... All large-scale hostels should be closed. This will take at least five years' (Scottish Executive 2000, p.31).

These recommendations were, in effect, endorsed by the Homelessness Task Force when it reported in 2001 (Homelessness Task Force c.2001) and are in the process of implementation at the time of writing. This will not apply to many of the establishments featured in the Quarriers study, however, because the Review Team Report also recommended that: 'Specialist supported small-scale units should be provided for those with acute or chronic needs' (Scottish Executive 2000, p.31).

Rather than closing, therefore, it is likely that most of the hostels for young homeless people will remain open for many years to come, although they will refine their remit, so that they are able to provide a service for those whose acute needs have caused them to be excluded from other forms of provision. Examples might include young people with addiction problems and those who self-harm. This is not necessarily good news in view of the negative aspects of accommodating groups of young people together under one roof (see Chapter 7). These factors could potentially negate the benefits of providing skilled focused assistance to some of the most vulnerable young people.

It is clear, however, that services for young homeless people are not considered to be accommodation services, pure and simple. Assistance or support of a more or less specialised or intense nature is an essential component of all these services and we must now consider what the parameters of support are in practice, and indeed what the term means.

What is support?

The issue of support has come to dominate the response to homelessness, because of its link to accommodation in many forms of provision. Support is a vital, but often ill-defined, element of the services and there is often a great deal of confusion about the meaning of the term. Clapham and Evans (2000) identified six categories of support, including self-actualisation and personal skills, such as maintaining a healthy lifestyle, as well as help with practical skills, including the ability to obtain accommodation, manage personal finances and look after oneself.

Almost all of the young people participating in the Quarriers study were receiving several of these categories of support, often from more than one source. Young people were asked directly to whom they would turn if they needed help with a problem, and family members and friends featured just as prominently in their responses as professional helpers of all kinds (see Chapter 6).

The attitude of young people to the support received from staff contains the full spectrum of approval/disapproval one might expect. Some were, at times, frankly negative:

If ye see the staff in here, they make a big issue oot a things. (Young man aged 20)

Others were more discriminating:

Some of the staff are quite good. ***'s good, but some of them are hopeless. (Young woman aged 17)

Extremely positive responses could also, not infrequently, be heard:

Aye, my social worker. I think she's a brilliant help. I've also goat a drink counsellor. He's amazing. I've also a befriender, from [name of agency], who helps me a lot and gives me something tae dae. (Young woman aged 19)

When asked how help for young homeless people could be improved, a number of the young people in the Quarriers study referred to professional support services. In some cases, they focused on the support arrangements that operated within hostels and supported accommodation projects themselves, notably the 'key work' system prevailing in many of the hostels for young people, wherein each resident is assigned to a specific member of staff, or 'key worker', to help them address their own needs and problems.

> I think they need more staff. There's not enough staff members to know what's going on, with people. You should have two key workers, so if one's on holiday, you could speak to the other one. (Young woman aged 17)

A young woman, aged 21, expounded on the importance of the key work system, as she saw it:

> Because of key worker, building relationships, assisting in helping young person get exactly what they want in life with regarding to personal situation, education and employment, dreams and aspirations, people would be set up in good stead, an aim which is achievable to them and makes them feel worthwhile. Key worker sessions are central to keeping developing young people to sustain a tenancy, outwith hostels.

Several studies have highlighted the importance of the key work system in the provision of effective support. Allen (2003) also emphasises the need for maximum continuity of key work. Philip and Shucksmith (2004) considered 'mentoring relationships' in the widest sense as planned supportive relationships between vulnerable young people and adults, who might be paid key workers or volunteer mentors or befrienders. They found that it made little difference to the young person whether the mentor was paid or a volunteer but that sustaining the relationship and managing its closure was of vital importance. An abrupt or insensitive closure could undermine its benefits and reinforce feelings of rejection. A strong note of caution must be sounded here, however. Although the young person is chiefly interested in the quality of the relationship, and the benefits that may accrue from it, paid professionals cannot be the young person's friend. Conflicts of role will inevitably arise, leaving the young person disillusioned, and in order to perform the role adequately, an element of professional 'distance' must be maintained.

There was a wide variation in young people's desired style of support from staff:

> If they would put mair trust in ye and spend mair time wi ye. (Young woman aged 20)

> Somebody to give me a boot up the arse. (Young woman aged 23)

Some young people's desired model of support extended beyond their current situation:

> To assist them when they get a house, so they don't lose it again and end up back in the homeless scene. They should have a befriender, or someone that comes round to see them, if they've got no pals. (Young woman aged 21)

These comments tended to focus upon descriptions of a support style that could easily apply to anyone, rather than specialised services geared to the needs of young homeless people. Fitzpatrick (2000) attempted to assess the level of vulnerability of young people participating in her study by considering the nature of the support that each required and found that, on that basis, most could be considered 'vulnerable' rather than 'ordinary'. She based her assessment of their support needs on the services they were receiving at a given moment in time whereas it is quite likely that different conclusions might be reached by other professionals, or the young people themselves.

Hutson and Liddiard (1994), however, argue that vulnerability can arise from the circumstances in which young people find themselves, often denying them access to the supportive resources available to the more fortunate, rather than from special characteristics or deficiencies inherent in the individuals themselves. The comments of the young people participating in the Quarriers study seem to indicate that, with some justification, they regard themselves as 'ordinary young people in extraordinary circumstances'.

Young people who don't want support

Children and young people generally do not consider it appropriate or necessary to access formal or professional forms of support, unless they are in extreme circumstances and have no one else to turn to. Although it might seem obvious that the condition of homelessness qualifies as an example of 'extreme circumstances', this may not fit with homeless young people's own perception of ordinariness described above. If an individual sees him- or herself as having become homeless through a combination of poor decision-making and bad luck, then it may not occur to them that they need the support of professional care-givers. If such a notion is suggested to them by others, they may reject it as absurd, or even insulting.

In these circumstances, which are by no means uncommon, young people are much more likely to turn to friends or family members for advice or help with a problem and this provides the most likely explanation for the opinions summarised in Table 6.2 in Chapter 6. When young people had experience of professional help, they generally valued it highly, but those who hadn't experienced it often couldn't imagine themselves doing so. The problem is that at least some of those rejecting the notion of professional support could almost certainly benefit greatly from it.

There is no easy answer to this conundrum other than ultimately to accept the individual's own assessment of what they need and can accept. This is, in my view, a sound general principle, although there are, of course, important exceptions. Whilst the conventional wisdom is generally true that one has to want help in order to benefit from it, there are situations where a young person's safety or the safety of others may be compromised if action is not taken. An obvious example of this is the possibility of an acute mental health problem, part of which may involve a degree of suppression of the young person's insight, so that this individual may not be able to accept that he or she requires urgent help. Mental health services and supporting legislation provide the necessary element of compulsion in extreme cases, and referrals must be made in these situations, if necessary without the young person's consent and involvement.

Those young people who are not in such serious difficulties cannot profitably be forced to accept formal support against their will. The staff of homelessness services with whom they come into contact may be able to provide what is needed in an unobtrusive way, via the development of a positive relationship, but the other alternative is the provision of non-professional support. The potential benefits of befriending and mentoring are mentioned elsewhere in this book, as is the possibility of 'buddy' systems, linking the young person with a positive support person of their own age group. Young people may also rebel against this notion, arguing that they prefer to find their own friends naturally, or seek out family members. Of course they are free to do so, but as in other walks of life, the most accessible friend is not always the most reliable or the one who has one's best interests at heart. Even though rejection is always a possibility, workers involved with young homeless people must always try to provide access to a support person who is known to be reliable and is proven to have good intentions.

Specialised support

We have already made reference, on several occasions, to more specialised forms of support. A 23-year-old young woman who had experienced rough sleeping felt that:

> They should have more drop-in centres for women, because there aren't many, i.e. showers, bathing, eating.

A sizeable body of literature supports her view, by identifying various subgroups within the homeless population with special support needs, including homeless mothers (Hinton and Gorton 1999) and young people with mental health problems, particularly prevalent amongst those with experience of residential care as children (McCann *et al.* 1996). The same 23-year-old young woman also specifically referred to her background of care:

> 'I'd like to see more things done for young people 15 onwards, coming out of care, or kids on the run'.

Issues linked to mental health difficulties and also to troubled early childhoods include self-harm and eating disorders. Addiction problems are now commonplace amongst young homeless people and, as we have already seen in Chapter 8, present major challenges to services. The support of young people struggling with any of these issues requires some specialist knowledge and skills and specialist services may be available for onward referral, although the 'postcode lottery' applies to some extent here, in that not all of the services may be available in every area. There is a fine balance to be drawn here for workers in services for young homeless people. On one hand it is important that staff engaging with these complex issues have the necessary skills and knowledge since it is possible to do more harm than good. On the other hand, it is equally important that workers do not become frightened of this complexity and distance themselves from young people. To do so might well leave some young people less supported than those with less complex and acute needs.

In many areas of the UK services are administered on what is termed the 'NHS model'. Young people with complex difficulties are likely to find themselves engaged with at least one and perhaps several specialist agencies in different parts of the city. They are expected to keep regular appointments at these locations and, in some cases, as we have seen with opiate addiction (Chapter 8), this may be so onerous that it takes over their lives to a large extent. Homelessness itself involves many obligations in terms of engagement with the housing and benefits systems. Young people often do not respond well to a situation where numerous and complex demands are placed upon them in order to inch towards the resolution of what may seem an insoluble problem. Hence, a degree of integration, in the delivery of such services, has proved valuable in terms of the engagement and retention of clients. An example of this is the provision of addiction services peripatetically, or within hostels and supported accommodation services.

The separation of housing and support

One important drawback of much of the support currently offered to young homeless people is that it is tied to the provision of accommodation. Many young homeless people have complex housing histories with a large number of changes of address, so the likelihood at present is that any supportive link that has been established through these services is likely to be broken with each move. This can engender a sense of insecurity amongst young people that was apparent in some of the responses of those involved in the Quarriers research and that can hardly have been helpful to them:

> It's not the staff that get to me, it's the system. When you get pulled in the office, you feel it's a big problem. They make a big deal about stupid things. This should be a stable place, you shouldn't feel like you're going to get kicked out. (Young woman aged 20)

Fitzpatrick (2000) draws similar conclusions from her study, suggesting that 'floating support' that is not tied to residence in any particular establishment, or location, may be the way forward for these services.

The advent of Supporting People funding in 2003 has provided the impetus for the development of a number of new floating support services and this, together with the development of a programme aimed at closing hostels for the homeless in Glasgow, provides a favourable climate, in Glasgow at least, for a gradual change in the pattern of services in the years to come.

The majority of the services being utilised by young people involved in the Quarriers study are still likely to feature prominently for many more years, however. They include hostels, where young people may be admitted for a short period of assessment when they become homeless, and supported accommodation services where young people may stay for a longer period of time, perhaps up to two years. These services allow the young person a varying degree of independence, with the allocation of a single flat or bed-sitter, but with a staff presence, on site, usually on a 24-hour basis. There is one important difference between these services and those which follow the housing support model. The control over occupancy lies with the staff, usually via an occupancy agreement of some kind. Staff can enter a young person's room or flat, and even evict a young person at any time, if they have reasonable grounds for doing so. In order to ensure, as far as possible, the safety and security of other residents and staff, this ultimate sanction is regarded as necessary. If it did not exist, the likely result would be a much more conservative policy on admissions. Services would be reluctant to take any chances with the very vulnerable and sometimes volatile young people who, arguably, have the greatest need for the support that such services can provide. Housing support gives the resident the legal rights of a tenant and, while intensive staff support may be provided, the resident is under no legal obligation to accept it, or even admit members of staff to their dwelling.

Services that rely solely upon housing support, even relatively intensive support, have not coped well with young people at the extreme upper end of the spectrum of vulnerability, including those with serious addiction problems and chaotic patterns of drug use. It has been found that a higher level of staff control than this model normally allows is required to ensure the safety and security of residents and to give them the chance to make positive progress protected from some of the pressures to which they may have succumbed in the past. Of course, independent living remains the goal for all young people using homelessness services, but the speed at which they can progress towards it varies according to the complexity of their problems. Good and accurate assessment that can identify, as soon as possible after they present as homeless, the various supports that will enable them to achieve optimum progress towards independence is also, therefore, vital.

Learning points

- Almost all homeless young people want their own independent tenancy.

- Youth homelessness cannot be irradicated without an adequate supply of suitable, affordable housing.

- Excessively long stays in transitional accommodation militate against progress towards independence.

- Support is an essential element of services for young homeless people and works best if 'personalised', i.e. adapted to the specific needs and wishes of the individual. This is often successfully accomplished through a 'key worker' system.

- Young people also benefit greatly from positive relationships with reliable adults and these cannot be provided solely by staff. This is especially true when young people reject professional support as 'unnecessary'.

- Specialist support works best when integrated with other services and provided 'on site'.

- Young homeless people are likely to move several times during their period of homelessness. Consistent support should continue through these changes and not fracture with each change of accommodation.

- Housing support may not provide an adequate service for some very vulnerable young people on its own. Those with severe addiction problems, for example, may need some time in a staffed facility first.

- As in all forms of care, a full and accurate assessment of need at the earliest possible stage is vital.

- User involvement in the planning of future services in vital to their chances of success.

Conclusion

Government agencies are currently paying a good deal of attention to the question of housing supply, which is most welcome, if somewhat overdue. Understandably, the tightest focus tends to be on the south-east of England, where over-crowding in the most general sense has become an issue widely recognised by the general public. However, housing shortages apply to a greater or lesser extent to almost every other part of the UK. This is particularly apparent when one looks beyond the need for more family homes, which is inevitably the first priority, to smaller segments of the housing market, such as affordable social housing suitable for young single people. It is the supply of this type of housing that impacts upon the plight of the young homeless people. A truism so important it is worth repeating is that the problem of youth homelessness cannot be solved without a significant increase in the availability of affordable housing suitable to their needs.

Housing supply alone cannot solve the problem. This is evidenced by the 'revolving door syndrome' whereby young people often lose the tenancies of suitable homes almost as soon as they obtain them. We have seen how developing adults acquire a range of practical skills and a degree of emotional resilience that together make up the qualities needed to become a competent householder, able to sustain a tenancy in the long-term. These skills and competencies cannot be taught by the provision of a short training course. More fortunate members of our society tend to be mentored by their parents or other family members over an extended period of time. Young homeless people themselves emphasise the high value that they place on support that most closely replicates this situation. We have seen how support can take many different forms, but, in the broadest sense, it must form the twin focus, along with housing supply of any strategy aimed at ameliorating, reducing or ending youth homelessness.

References

Allen, M. (2003) *Into the Mainstream. Care Leavers Entering Work, Education and Training.* York: Joseph Rowntree Foundation.

Bannister, J., Dell, M., Donnison, D., Fitzpatrick, S. and Taylor, R. (1993) *Homeless Young People in Scotland: The Role of the Social Work Services.* Edinburgh: HMSO.

Clapham, D. and Evans, A. (2000) 'Social exclusion: The case of homelessness.' In I. Anderson and D. Sim (eds) *Social Exclusion and Housing: Context and Challenges.* Coventry: Chartered Institute of Housing.

Fitzpatrick, S. (2000) *Young Homeless People.* Basingstoke: Macmillan.

Hinton, T. and Gorton, S. (1999) 'Forgotten mothers.' *Community Care* 1–7 July.

Homelessness Task Force (c.2001) *Homelessness: An Action Plan for Prevention and Effective Response.* Task Force final report. Edinburgh: Stationery Office.

Hutson, S. and Liddiard, M. (1994) *Youth Homelessness: The Construction of a Social Reality.* Basingstoke: Macmillan.

McCann, J.B., James, A. Wilson, S. and Dunn, G. (1996) 'Prevalence of psychiatric disorders in young people in the care system.' *British Medical Journal 313,* 1529–1530.

Philip, K. and Shucksmith, J. (2004) *Supporting Vulnerable Young People. Exploring Planned Mentoring Relationships.* CRFR Research Briefing 19. Edinburgh: Centre for Research on Families and Relationships.

Scottish Executive (2000) *Helping Homeless People.* The Report of the Glasgow Review Team to the Homelessness Task Force. Edinburgh: Scottish Executive.

10

The Human Factor

*What Works when Responding
to Adolescent Behaviour?*

Any conversation with young people using hostels, supported accommodation projects, or other services for the homeless is likely to turn to members of staff and young people's opinion of them. It is a human characteristic to personalise our feelings about what is going on in our lives, good and bad, in respect of the people to whom we are closest at the time. Staff and residents of a service for young homeless people often spend a good deal of time together and intense relationships can develop. The methods of work employed in social care services also tend to use relationships as a primary working tool, although the users of the service may have varying awareness of what is happening and why. Many young homeless people are experienced users of services of this kind and have a keen and sometimes critical awareness of the skills and shortcomings of the staff. Others can surprise one with their innocence, regarding all adults with whom they come into contact as potential friends.

Whatever the context, relationships between staff and young people within services can vary enormously but are of immense importance to those sharing the experience of homelessness from different perspectives. Positive trusting relationships permit successful work which really helps young people. Such relationships must be able to survive tough encounters dealing with difficult issues, because this is the nature of the work. Although skills in the making and sustaining of such relation-ships can be learned, there is no infallible formula, so it has to be accepted that some young people and some staff will simply not get on.

This chapter is about the nature of relationships between staff and young people. We will consider the recorded views of both young people and staff on this subject and seek to deconstruct some of the essential elements and common pitfalls, focusing above all on what works and how things can be improved.

Vulnerable or ordinary young people?

Ever since youth homelessness emerged as a major social issue in the UK in the late 1980s, political ideology about the causes of the phenome-non has played a major part in determining the nature of practical responses to it. For the individual worker in a service addressing the needs of these young people, their personal understanding of the wider phenomenon will have a major influence on their attitude and approach.

The popularity of underclass theory among conservative political circles in the UK may have influenced the decision to remove state benefit entitlements from 16- and 17-year-olds, a decision which other analysts have considered to be one of the main causes of youth home-lessness. Jones (1997) goes further and argues that New Right theorists persuaded the Conservative Government to remove the welfare safety net in a vain attempt to reduce homelessness by regulating demand. If young people were leaving home and becoming homeless as a rational choice, then moving the economic goal posts so that they could only survive by remaining in the parental home would, it was argued, reduce homelessness.

Structuralist and post-structualist writers subsequently argued that the impact of social deprivation and state intervention limited personal responsibility to varying extents and prevented these ideologically-driven policies from achieving their desired result (see also Chapter 3).

The popular press constantly rehearses the contention that young poeple today, or a significant minority of them, are notably different from those of former times. This is particularly apparent in the reporting of gang violence, knife crime, or other manifestations of shockingly antisocial behaviour, but homelessness and its supposed causes are sometimes drawn in as well. Whether the nature of 'deviant' youth behaviour is changing or whether it is qualitatively much the same as it has always been is a moot point but, as discussed in Chapters 2 and 3, it is clear that young homeless people are diverse in their characteristics. Although some highly delinquent young people may be found amongst them and many many more are the product of dysfuntional backgrounds, all also have choices and the potential to change and grow.

Staff–resident relationships

The young people involved in the Quarriers research (see Appendix) were all resident in a hostel or supported accommodation project that was staffed and inevitably had some institutional features. None had their own tenancy at the time of their involvement. In these circumstances, the detailed workings of the hostel or project concerned and the varied skills and approaches of staff assumed a great importance to them. Comments referring to the relative shortage of staff and the ways that it impacted upon young people through, for example, limiting the individual attention they received featured in many of the interviews:

> My key worker 'R' who is very helpful and made me feel welcome. I feel at ease with her. I don't see her often enough but that's because they're under staffed. (Young woman aged 18)

It is undoubtedly true that many hostels are understaffed, but the range of different models of provision for homeless people is immense (Neale 1997). In the Quarriers questionnaire, agencies were asked how many of their staff were engaged in providing direct services to young people but unfortunately the responses to this question do not, on their own, provide a sound basis for comparison.

A number of quite negative comments were made by young people about the way staff interacted with residents. A young woman aged 17, for example, said:

> The way some o' them speak to you, it's fucking out of order.

Another young woman, aged 23 commented:

> There are a few good ones that can actually do their job description. Others are just in it for the money, trying to get a title to their name.

Some comments smacked of youthful rebelliousness and could equally well have been made about any living situation:

> I want out as soon as possible. Staff are doing my head in. (Young man aged 20)

If the word 'staff' was substituted by the word 'parents', one can easily imagine the same comment being made about the family home, since young people in transition inevitably set their sights upon the freedom of their own home. Resentment at the restrictions involved in conforming to someone else's set of rules is commonplace in these circumstances.

Only 11 of the 58 agencies responding to the agency questionnaire said that they had a formal code of conduct covering relations between staff and young people. Unfortunately none responded to an invitation to enclose a copy of their code when returning the postal questionnaire. Casson and Johnson (1996) describe the establishment of a quality assurance system in an agency providing services for young homeless people. When they asked both young people and staff to suggest areas for the establishment of quality standards, there was a clear difference between the approaches of these two groups. The young people's suggestions were more specific and largely to do with the direct relationship between themselves and staff, whereas the agency standards were more to do with equal rights and fairness. A similar dichotomy can be discerned between young people's and agency views in this study.

A 20-year-old young man was a little more analytical in his comments:

> Communication with the staff should be improved, they're always busy! I wish the staff wouldn't be so judgemental.

All the conflicts inherent in the adolescent desire for both safety and independence were evident in the comments of yet another 20-year-old young man, when he said:

> I think clear instructions from staff would make things better. I think the staff should get off the residents' backs. If there's a little bit of dust on the carpet they say you've not hoovered properly.

Rules and regulations are a common feature of most hostels and supported accommodation projects, but the detailed nature of the rules, which ones are considered crucial and how rigorously they are enforced, is frequently a moot point (Neale 1997). On the other hand, many subjects made extremely positive comments about staff. For example, a 21-year-old young woman simply said:

> The staff's really good

The considered view of a 25-year-old young man was:

> I think there should be more hostels available like this one. I don't think they can do much more than they are doing now. Any pattern of behaviour can only be changed if the person wants to change it

A 21-year-old young woman had also obviously given this matter a great deal of thought:

> I remember I didn't like a member of staff in [name of agency]. She was never any good at giving discipline appropriately. Always had a tone of voice that got on my goat to say the least! Felt I wasn't treated as a person. But one day I met her at the bus stop and we started chatting for ten minutes before the bus came. She seemed like a different person; stopped being a member of staff dictating rules and procedures and saw her as a person. I thought this was similar to other staff. Staff are different outwith the hostel.

The institutional aspects of current services

A number of young people participating in the Quarriers research made some quite powerful comments about what might be described as the 'institutional' aspects of the hostels or supported accommodation projects in which they were living.

> [Name of hostel], eight months, I think. I think it's a shit hole. For a start they have goat rules, which they don't go by. The condition of the place is nae up tae much. (Young woman aged 18)

> [Name of agency], supported lodging, three month. It's good, too many rules, i.e. got to attend college courses, be up for 10am for meetings every morning, have got to be in for 11 pm nightly. (Young woman aged 23)

Another 23-year-old young woman spoke with a degree of insight, but also bitterness about how the institutionalism of services had affected her:

They shouldn't have kept me in the institution for so long because my independence was taken away from me, to end up dependent on them. If you're treated like a wain then you'll act like one.

On the other hand, another young woman, aged 19, reflected on the higher level of independence that she felt was afforded her by the supported accommodation project where she was living:

[Name of project], it's actually residential care. You get all your food, toiletries for free. You have your own flat in a close. I've been there for three weeks. Before that I was staying in [name of another agency] and then my mum's. I really, really like the place as it's my own flat.

Consultation with users of a service is one way to break down institutional barriers of the type hinted at in many of these young people's comments. In the questionnaire, agencies were asked whether they consulted with young people who used their services, on a formal or informal basis. Of the 58 responding agencies, 32 said that they did consult regularly on a formal basis, while 29 claimed that they did so informally. This can be considered a strongly positive response when compared with many of the other responses to the questionnaire. For example, only 13 agencies said that they actively promoted contact between young people and their families, whilst only 16 said that they encouraged peer support of each other by young people and one said that they actively discouraged it.

Consulting with young people and involving residents in the running of institutions, in a way that gives them the opportunity to make decisions about aspects of the regime that are important to them, is of course easier said than done. There are many barriers to involvement (Fitzpatrick, Hastings and Kintrea 1998), including the complexity of processes, the formality of meeting etiquette and the jargon-ridden language that is often used. It must also be accepted that adults do not always believe that young people have a legitimate role to play in complex strategic discussions. On the other hand, young people may often lack the confidence or the interest needed to become involved effectively, and territorialism, cynicism and disaffection are all attitudes that can get in the way. Nevertheless, Fitzpatrick *et al.* (1998) found that there was far less cynicism than expected and that there was no evidence that young people who participated were considered 'uncool' by their peers.

One of the agencies involved in the Quarriers study organised a conference in 2005, attended by representatives from nine hostels and housing support projects for young people, operated by the agency. One of the outcomes of this conference was the establishment of a permanent group. This group is formally constituted, with office bearers elected from within the delegate membership and supported by staff from the agency. It has a remit to represent residents' views on the way services are run within the agency, to engage with relevant issues externally, and has already become active in these areas. The group also links into a wider inclusion network within the agency and beyond, representing a range of different client groups.

Ideas for improvement

Very little is known about how residents feel about living in hostels or supported accommodation and, in particular, to what extent they sense that they have rights, control and choice. Or do they feel stigmatised, disempowered and excluded (Neale 1997)? The evidence from the Quarriers study is that the picture is very mixed and a young person's perception of the overall regime of a hostel is often coloured by their relationship with a particular member of staff. Writing about children's homes, Emond (2002) argues that young people are, in reality, far from powerless. On the contrary, they 'manage' the resident group through a complex set of ongoing negotiations, whereby power and status within the group is allocated. Furthermore, the allocation of these roles is constantly shifting, usually without the involvement, or even the awareness, of the staff.

Most young people in transitional accommodation occupy their residences under licence, rather than a lease, and therefore do not enjoy normal tenancy rights. Agencies have traditionally taken the view that the risk of difficult behaviour of various kinds is so high when dealing with such vulnerable young people that it is necessary to reserve the power to evict a trouble-maker instantly (see also Chapter 9). The alternative would involve going through the time-consuming process of notice to quit and court order that would be required if full tenancy rights were granted. Although a hostel might remain stable for months at a time, its eviction policy would, almost inevitably, prompt some comment during more troubled times:

> They should stop evicting people fur the slightest wee things. (Young woman aged 20)

Young people are often enthusiastic about the opportunity to express their ideas for improvement, in relation to staff and institutional living, as in other respects. A 16-year-old, asked about ways in which services could be improved said

> Give them a chance to prove themselves and show people what they can do. Give them a bit more respect.

A 20-year-old young woman presented a quite sophisticated and well thought through plan to overcome the institutionalisation inherent in the system:

> I think residents at the [name of hostel] should be graded on their behaviour, and ability to cope with their own life. If they could prove they can do that then why not allow them special privileges. The curfew, for example, I don't know... It should be the ones that misbehave that get less privileges and the ones that do behave should be left alone. A plan should be made up for people in here, like a life plan, like what they want to do and what they want to achieve in their life. That's what most people in here need. The key workers should be there to help them follow this and to motivate them, every day.

Another young woman aged 18 had a different set of recommendations that were more to do with relationships than the system:

> I think residents and staff should have regular meetings and group work activities so we could all get to know each other better and discuss all problems in the hostel and how to improve them. If we get on with the staff it makes things easier. They should have workshops like cooking sessions, guitar playing, art. We've goat a mini-bus, we should dae something with it. Look at the weather. It wouldnae cost much tae go tae a museum or a beach or a kick aboot in the park.

A 19-year-old young woman with a very troubled background commented:

> I think the staff need more training regarding issues around sexual abuse. Staff state they don't discuss these issues and refer me to see one member of staff only.

The comments recorded above are only a small and necessarily unrepresentative selection, but do serve to illustrate the intense and critical interest displayed by young people using these services. The researchers working on the Quarriers study found young people more willing to talk about services and how they could be improved than any other subject. The potential to involve young people in the governance and management of services is clearly considerable and underdeveloped.

Staff qualifications and experience

The advent of a central registration with a remit to establish registration criteria and then to register all categories of social work and social care staff has brought issues around staff qualification to the fore. Agencies were asked in the Quarriers postal questionnaire about the minimum qualification and experience requirements for their basic grade staff. Two agencies stated that they had no minimum qualification, whilst only six and five respectively specified SVQ/NVQ level three and HNC in Social Care. Other agencies made mention of a mixed bag of more or less relevant areas of qualification, including counselling, youth work, degree-level community education, nursery nursing, teaching and social work. At the margins, the variation between agencies, with regard to their qualification requirements, was quite extreme, ranging from 'Desirable, but not essential', through 'SVQ3, ideally, HNC, NNEB', to 'Essential: HNC Social Care (or equivalent); desirable: DipSW (or equivalent)'.

At the time of writing, the Scottish Social Services Council has not specified registration requirements for workers in residential establishments for young homeless people (hostels) and no timetable for them to do so has been established. In 2005, however, registration criteria for workers in housing support services were published. These requirements will eventually apply to workers in many of the newer services for young homeless people, where they are supported within their own tenancies, although they also apply to similar support services for other client groups. The minimum registration requirements are the SVQ/NVQ level two, 'Principles of Care' unit, if accompanied by one of a number of housing qualifications, or SVQ/NVQ level two, in Care, Direct Care or Health and Social Care, on its own. This may be compared with the requirements for residential workers with adults with a disability (SVQ/NVQ level three) or residential workers with children (SVQ/NVQ level three and HNC).

The situation in England and Wales is somewhat different. The regulator here is the General Social Care Council (GSCC) and the principle of registration was established by The Care Standards Act (2000). 'Social worker' became a protected title in 2005, in the sense that no one was allowed to claim that title, thereafter, unless they met the registration criteria and had been formally registered by the GSCC. Student social workers are also required to register. An extensive consultation was conducted to determine the subsequent priorities for registration and it was decided that domiciliary care workers should be the next group to be registered. The rationale for this was that domiciliary workers are mostly unsupervised and have a high level of contact with service users, in their own homes. This includes young people who have experienced homelessness and who are being supported in their own tenancies. Although the UK Government has indicated that it intends, over time, to ask the GSCC to register all categories of social care workers, including residential workers, the present situation diverges significantly from that prevailing in Scotland. The registration of the estimated 200,000 domiciliary workers in England and Wales is scheduled to begin early in 2008 but as yet there is no timetable for registering residential workers.

In view of the complexities involved in the resettlement and support of young homeless people, it is hard to rationalise the justification for such a low qualification threshold. Most of the sub-set of 12 agencies participating in the study made it clear that their staff were dealing with extremely difficult and demanding issues on a routine basis. On this basis, it is possible to argue that the qualification standard should be at least equivalent to that for residential workers with children. Of course, there are many practical and financial difficulties involved in moving to a fully qualified workforce, starting from a relatively low baseline, and these difficulties may have informed the decision. It would seem, however, that a substantial programme of training will be required to overcome the extremely mixed pattern currently prevailing in order to meet even the low criteria that have been set.

The minimum experience requirement for basic grade staff specified by four agencies responding to the questionnaire was two or more years experience of working with young people, whilst a further ten agencies identified the same area of work experience as crucial, but without specifying a period of time. Other areas of experience mentioned by single agencies were mental health, addiction, homelessness, work with abuse survivors and work with ethnic minorities. Once again, the variation between agencies in this regard was considerable, governed to some extent by the role of the agency and the degree of specialisation inherent within it. Hence, an agency offering a service for homeless female abuse survivors required experience of: 'work with survivors and related issues', while an agency operating a direct-access emergency hostel looked for 'some experience of working with young socially excluded individuals'.

Agencies were asked whether they provided in-service training for their staff which included the values and principles of work with young people. Eighteen agencies responded in the affirmative and a wide range of training topics was specified. Those most frequently mentioned were: child sexual abuse/child protection training (four), group work (three), values and principles (three), basic youth work (two) and housing issues for young people (two). There was some variation, and while the smaller agencies understandably outsourced their staff training, some others offered quite extensive menus of courses. One such agency listed the following courses: 'Values in Social Care, Reflective Practices, Mental Health Issues, Understanding/Handling of Aggressive and Violent Behaviour including Self-Harm'.

Although the situation is gradually improving, it seems clear that expectations of staff in the field of homelessness, in terms of qualification and experience, are considerably lower than in most other branches of social care. In the past, work with people with learning disabilities has enjoyed the same sort of 'Cinderella status' but may now be as much as ten years ahead. The status and remuneration of staff working with young homeless people is in urgent need of enhancement, because improvements in morale, motivation and effectiveness will come in the wake of such changes.

Confidentiality

One of the key concerns of young people using services for the homeless is the question of whether information about them that is known by staff will be kept strictly confidential. Any perceived failure to maintain the standard of confidentiality that a young person considers appropriate is likely to draw a strong reaction and may colour relationships with staff and other important adults in the young person's life:

> Fuck talking to the staff, you can't tell them anything without everybody else knowing. (Young woman aged 17)

Residents are often curious about exactly what records are kept about them, and openness is undoubtedly the best policy, since fantasies about what might be recorded are invariably worse than reality. A very reasonable suggestion was made by a young man aged 25:

> I'd like to be able to access the information [name of agency] have on me with regard to the computer (under supervision of course).

Many services deploy an open records policy, which not only has the benefit of helping to engender trust between residents and staff, but also imposes the useful discipline of recording in a way that one would be happy to have read by young people themselves.

The principle of conditional confidentiality, whereby confidentiality may be breached in certain extreme circumstances, is likely to be familiar and acceptable to most of the young people through previous contact with social work agencies. Hence it should be made clear to young people at the outset that confidentiality cannot be guaranteed absolutely. If information is received that a young person's safety and wellbeing is under threat, for example, a disclosure of ongoing abuse, then the member of staff must be free to take the relevant steps to protect the young person and cannot be bound by absolute assurances of confidentiality. A number of examples where absolute confidentiality was initially felt to be necessary to gain young people's trust can be found in the literature. In most cases there is an evolution from absolute to conditional confidentiality, and just such a process is described in a study about research involving children (France, Bendelow and Williams 2000). When face-to-face work with young people commenced, it was quickly established that conditional confidentiality was indeed familiar to most of the young people involved and was not an issue of concern to them. A statement of informed consent was developed for all participants in the Quarriers project and peer researchers were given training to enable them to understand its importance and explain it to others.

Concern about the observance of confidentiality more generally is often, however, a major and continuing concern. It must be said that many young people have very little faith in assurances of confidentiality by professionals of all types.

Safety

Most young people entering services for the homeless have been traumatised to a greater or lesser extent. The need for a secure place to stay is a primary human requirement. The fear and anxiety that any person experiences in the face of the absence of such security is all-consuming, unless it is a situation with which they are already familiar. This is true of people of any age but the impact is likely to be even more extreme on young people, still at an age when it would be more usual for them to be living in the family home. Researchers have sought to determine the median age of leaving home in the wider population. Jones (1997), for example, found it to be 21.9 for males and 20.0 for females, although 30 per cent of males and 38 per cent of females still living with their parents had previously lived away from home for a period of six months or more since the age of 16. In other words, the most common pattern applying in our society is that young people leave for 'trial' periods at college, or for other purposes away from home, keeping the door of the family home open for them to return, until they are finally ready for full independence at some point in their 20s.

Most young homeless people have a very different experience and one for which they can hardly have been prepared. They are usually forced to leave home, with little planning or warning, their departure often precipitated by violent or traumatic events. They are also significantly younger, on average, than most young people, when they finally achieve independence. Not only is the experience of homelessness traumatic in its own right, but it is more often than not accompanied by other events that can only increase the fear and insecurity experienced by the young person. We have already seen (Chapter 6), how frequently family breakdown, sometimes involving violent conflict, plays a part in precipitating homelessness. Those of us fortunate enough to have made a planned move from a secure family, to our own timescale, can scarcely understand what this must be like.

For all of these reasons, the provision of a safe environment should be the first priority for all transitional services for young homeless people. This is easier said than done, since such services can act as a magnet for all the undesirable influences of the street. Even young people who have led a relatively sheltered life prior to becoming homeless may be targets for those who would exploit them through involvement in prostitution or drug-dealing. As everyone knows, crime, often violent, is likely to follow in the wake of such involvement. This raises a complex set of issues which will be different for each service, but most importantly concern entry and access to residents. Non-residents must be strictly controlled and limited to those whom the resident wishes to have admitted and who mean the resident no obvious harm. Failure to observe this ground rule consistently will lead to young people feeling unsafe, and until this is rectified, progress towards independence is unlikely.

There are some situations where the safety of some more vulnerable young people can become a concern because of their own potentially self-injurious behaviour. The Quarriers research provides an account of the issues arising from the involvement as a peer researcher of a highly intelligent but troubled young woman, whose background included abuse, growing up in care and mental health and drug dependency problems. Despite the best and quite correct intention to treat every person as an individual and not to let perceptions of her become filtered through her problems there were many occasions when, unavoidably, these issues came to the fore, in the context of personal safety.

Inter-agency issues

Most homelessness agencies have developed comparatively recently, especially those specialising in providing services for young homeless people – which only emerged during the late 1980s. This is in contrast with most other branches of social work and social care. Services for children, for example, developed around 100 years earlier. Nevertheless, there are close parallels, in that most of the pioneering work was undertaken by the voluntary sector. Only once the need for services became accepted as a permanent necessity did the statutory sector move in as a major provider of services. In relation to services for the homeless, this process is still occurring and service development to date has been largely in the hands of voluntary organisations.

Charities are not truly independent in the way that they were in the nineteenth century. Instead of relying successfully on philanthropy driven by Christian conviction, the voluntary sector is now to a large extent reliant of funding from central and local government agencies, on whose behalf they provide services.

Since public authorities are required to obtain value for money in their commissioning activities, an element of competition is inevitable. Voluntary organisations are forced to bid competitively for service contracts and, as Hutson and Liddiard (1994) pointed out, this has led to the fragmentation of the overall pattern of services. Organisations that are forced to compete with one another have no incentive to work cooperatively together and, in the main, they do not. There has been a growing realisation, in recent years, that a much greater 'joining up' of working between services and agencies is essential if youth homelessness is to be reduced and ultimately eliminated.

Learning points

- The right kinds of relationship between staff and young people are difficult to achieve but vital to the success of services.

- These relationships will often reflect the adolescent struggle for independence, common to all young people of a similar age group.

- A key work system is helpful in the formation and maintenance of a positive professional relationship with at least one member of staff.

- All such relationships should operate within appropriate professional boundaries. There is often another separate need for a positive adult befriender or mentor, which cannot be met by staff.

- A consultative process, giving residents a stake in the running of services, is vital for a number of different reasons. It is useful in combating institutionalism, but also creates a favourable climate for the development of productive working relationships between staff and young people.

- Work with homeless young people frequently presents difficult challenges and requires high levels of skill. The status, remuneration, qualification level and experience of workers in these services must rise if services are to improve.

- Consistently high standards of confidentiality are essential to the formation and maintenance of positive professional relationships between young people and staff. Confidentiality should be conditional rather than absolute and informed by best practice in child protection.

- Homelessness almost invariably involves trauma, and young people need to feel safe if they are to address the problems that face them in a positive way. This will involve a confident staff presence exercising effective control over entry to the service by non-residents.

- Trust and security will be enhanced by the impression of a more 'joined up' and cooperative pattern of services between agencies. This would also enhance the impact and effectiveness of services.

Conclusion

Most of the young people participating in the Quarriers research expressed appreciation for the help they had received from the staff of services they had used and some, in time, became expert at negotiating the service labyrinth. Others fell by the wayside, especially if a particular service element was difficult to access, involved significant travel, or where a member of staff encountered by the young person seemed brusque or unsympathetic. During their time as a consumer of services some had also clearly become accustomed to viewing themselves as exceptionally needy or, to use the professional jargon, 'vulnerable', and one has to question whether such a self-image was ultimately helpful to their chances of rehabilitation.

Many of the young people, in this and other studies (Fitzpatrick 2000), put great emphasis on ordinary values, such as homeliness, safety, friendliness, a stimulating environment and the availability of simple support to help deal with any problem, when they assessed the qualities of the services they had experienced. Perhaps they were right, and, if so, this may provide a pointer to the way services for young homeless people should develop in the future.

References

Casson, S.F. and Johnson, M. (1996) *Total Quality in Services for Homeless Young People.* London: Centrepoint, unpublished.

Dickens, S. and Woodfield, K. (2004) *New Approaches to Youth Homelessness Prevention: A Qualitative Evaluation of the Safe in the City Cluster Schemes.* York: Joseph Rowntree Foundation.

Emond, R. (2002) 'Understanding the resident group.' *Scottish Journal of Residential Child Care 1.*

Fitzpatrick, S., Hastings, A. and Kintrea, K. (1998) *Including Young People in Urban Regeneration: A Lot to Learn?* Bristol: Policy Press.

France, A., Bendelow, G. and Williams, S. (2000) 'A "risky" business: Researching the health beliefs of children and young people.' In A. Lewis and G. Lindsay (eds) *Researching Children's Perspectives.* Buckingham: Open University Press.

Hall, T. (2001) *Better Times Than This: Youth Homelessness in Britain.* London: Pluto Press.

Hutson, S. and Liddiard, M. (1994) *Youth Homelessness. The Construction of a Social Reality.* Basingstoke: Macmillan.

Jones, G. (1997) 'Youth homelessness and the underclass.' In R. MacDonald (ed.) *Youth, the Underclass and Social Exclusion.* London: Routledge.

Neale, J. (1997) 'Hostels: A useful policy and practice response?' In R. Burrows, N. Pleace and D. Quilgars (eds) *Homelessness and Social Policy.* London: Routledge.

11

The Future of Services for the Homeless

The future of any social care service is of intense interest to those involved in delivering it but the future of youth homelessness services is of greater concern than most. This is because it is a relatively recent phenomenon. As we have seen in Chapter 3 there were very few visible young homeless people in the UK during the period between the end of the Second World War and the late 1980s. It was certainly not considered a sufficiently serious issue to collect statistics or commission specialised services. The phenomenon exploded into our consciousness in the late 1980s and almost immediately became the focus of a range of social policy initiatives aimed at dealing with the problem. Levels of public awareness have fluctuated in the years since then, but investment in services addressing the issue has remained relatively constant.

Despite this commitment of attention and resources, youth homelessness remains a serious issue for our society, and none of the many initiatives that we have described in this book can claim to have been wholly successful. In view of the recent history of youth homelessness in the UK, it is understandable that we should ask why, if it was virtually unknown in the relatively recent past, it cannot be eradicated in the future? In this concluding chapter we will try to assess the prospects of this happening in the foreseeable future. We will also consider what services could and should look like in the future if the chances of the reduction and/or elimination of youth homelessness are to be maximised.

Realistic expectations? Can youth homelessness be eliminated?

The future of services for young homeless people in the UK seems uncertain. In 2002, nfpSynergy's 'Charity Parliamentary Monitor' found that MPs' awareness of homelessness agencies was as low as 3 per cent, having dropped from 16 per cent two years earlier. This compares with 33 per cent awareness for the top-performing children's charity sector (Saxton and Evans 2002). Saxton and Evans also see homelessness agencies lagging behind the rest of the voluntary sector in two important respects: user involvement and ethnic minority issues. On one hand, they saw evidence of a future increase in the numbers of black and minority ethnic (BME) homeless people, caused by demographic changes within BME communities but, on the other hand, they noted the absence of mainstream, frontline organisations specifically focused on the needs of the BME homeless:

> Unless there is a greater emphasis on BME issues, particularly in London, from homelessness agencies, central and local government, the needs of a group of homeless people will not be incorporated into planning and service delivery. It will also be out of step with the wider social exclusion agenda. (Saxton and Evans 2002, p.22)

User involvement is also a highly significant factor in the development of services:

> User involvement, growing in importance in many parts of the voluntary sector, is the need to involve clients or users in the development and direction of the organisation. One agency director coming from outside the homelessness sector remarked on 'lack of formal mechanisms for user involvement and the distance homelessness agencies are behind other voluntary organisations'. (Saxton and Evans 2002, p.21)

They see two broad scenarios for ι. future of homelessness agencies and homeless people over the next decade. The first scenario envisages local authorities finding it difficult to meet their statutory obligations, due to housing shortages and limited resources. The need for more homes has consistently exceeded demand in recent years. Although the

UK Government announced an increase in the priority afforded to new house-building after Gordon Brown became Prime Minister, this shortage in the supply of housing looks likely to continue, especially in London and the South-East.

These difficulties are exacerbated by demographic changes, leading to an increased number of single person households and a greater proportion of elderly people within the population. These factors lead local authorities to bow to political and public pressures and shift their priorities away from the homeless in favour of more 'popular' deprived groups, such as the elderly. The second, more hopeful, scenario sees a reduction in the number of homeless presentations, due to low unemployment and the success of strategies to tackle poverty. The powers and duties placed upon local authorities by the Homelessness Act 2002 and the resources released through Supporting People act together to produce some creative and imaginative ways to tackle existing homelessness and prevent future homelessness, such as using empty homes. Substantial numbers of new affordable homes are being built (Saxton and Evans 2002).

These two scenarios are polarised, and it is clear that the response of homelessness agencies to individual young people holds the key to success or failure in the future. A survey found that new procedures introduced in response to the Homelessness Act 2002 in England had improved the situation for those accepted as being 'in priority need' but for those young people denied priority status, their experience of local authority homelessness services was, on the whole, negative (Shelter 2005). The situation in Scotland appeared to be somewhat better and the Scottish proposals to remove the priority need test entirely, by 2012, are probably the only realistic approach to ending homelessness for these young people. They are, however, likely to require an increase in investment in both accommodation and support services.

In the meantime, 'intentionality' – the principle enshrined in successive pieces of homelessness legislation, whereby local authorities are absolved from the responsibility to accommodate applicants deemed to have made themselves intentionally homeless – is inconsistently interpreted. The Shelter Survey (Shelter 2005) includes the example of 16- to 17-year-olds being considered intentionally homeless when problems had arisen due to the young person failing to follow their parents' rules. The freedom of local authorities to interpret the legislation in such an extreme manner acts in effect as 'a get-out clause' in relation to their statutory duties to young homeless people.

There is currently an increasing emphasis on the prevention of homelessness, following some concern that: 'the entire homelessness framework has created a self-perpetuating "homelessness industry"' (Shelter 2005, p.34).

The Homelessness Act 2002 placed a new obligation on English local authorities. In addition to their statutory duties they are now required to develop strategies to prevent homelessness from occurring in the first place. In particular, they are now encouraged to provide a wide range of advice and services to people seeking homelessness assistance. Recent official statistics reveal that 57 per cent of people accepted as homeless by local authorities in England became homeless because of relationship breakdown or having been asked to leave their accommodation by family or friends (Communities and Local Government 2007). As a result, mediation services are being promoted as a key strand of the new homelessness prevention approach. Of course, if reconciliation between a young person and their family can be safely accomplished, then the resources necessary to support such a process should be committed. To fail to do so would be to repeat the mistakes of the past since a major study of youth homelessness in Scotland included the development of mediation services amongst its recommendations as long ago as 1993 (Bannister *et al.* 1993).

Professionals working within the youth homelessness field emphasise the risks involved in returning to live at home for many young people (see Chapter 6). This does not negate the potential value of mediation in improving relations between young people and their families, thereby increasing the availability of ongoing support. It does, however, give rise to anxieties that mediation will be used by some local authorities as a means to remove young people from the homelessness system at all costs, by inducing them to return to a home that may not be safe for them to live in. In such an event young people may be placed in additional and unnecessary danger.

Other homelessness prevention services being developed include:

- **Rent deposit schemes**. Access to accommodation in the privately rented sector is facilitated for people unable to afford the initial payments that are usually required.

- **Supported lodgings schemes**. Members of the community provide a rented room within their own home for young people leaving their family home. A measure of practical and emotional support by the host family is usually anticipated, but the number of families willing and able to provide such a service has been found to be quite limited. Whilst it could form a valuable part of the overall mix of services, it is unlikely to make a major impact on youth homelessness on its own.

- **Sanctuary schemes**. A safe room is created in the home of a domestic violence victim and can act as a refuge if violence occurs. Such schemes could also prove relevant to young homeless people, because a significant proportion become homeless in flight from domestic violence.

Preventative work in schools, including programmes aimed at providing young people with the knowledge and information that they need to avoid becoming homeless, is increasingly being implemented. This will undoubtedly form an important part of future anti-homelessness strategies, but it is probably too early to fully evaluate its impact. It must also be noted that some high-risk individuals may be missed by these programmes due to their non-attendance at school. In Scotland, the most recent legislation also increased the period that local authorities have to consider an applicant as being threatened with homelessness from 28 days to two months. Many young people present as homeless in a crisis situation, however, and relatively few are likely to be able to notify the local authority of their impending threat of homelessness two months in advance.

All of the strategies aimed at ending or preventing homelessness, taken together, have the capability of success, if properly resourced and implemented. I therefore have few doubts in asserting that youth homelessness can be eliminated as anything other than a short-term phenomenon during an 'assessment period' while the necessary support services are being identified. The real question is whether youth homelessness will be afforded sufficient priority to attract the resources needed to bring this about. To some extent this will involve the refocusing of existing resources, rather than the wholesale provision of major new resources, but it is, nevertheless, a huge task and success or failure may ultimately depend upon the presence of the political will needed to ensure that the new statutory duties are enacted in practice, in the spirit as well as the letter of the legislation.

A model of future service provision

Services for young people who find themselves homeless have tended to become organised on what might be termed the 'health service model'. During a short period of assessment, their needs are identified and they are allocated to the service, or cluster of services, that most closely meets those needs. There is rarely any link with the young person's experiences as a child. A young person's behaviour may, for example, lead staff to suspect that he or she has learning disability, without them knowing that the young person may have been the subject of a record of needs during childhood. This will sometimes lead into a tortuous process whereby a service that may not actually exist is constructed, in order to provide the services that the young person needs. Where a young person's needs are complex or extreme he or she may be referred to one or more separate specialist services on an 'outpatient' basis.

Most of the young people participating in the Quarriers research (see Appendix) expressed appreciation for the help they had received from those services and may in time become expert at negotiating the service labyrinth. Others may fall by the wayside, especially if a particular service element is difficult to access, involves significant travel, or where the provider of the service seems, to the young person, brusque or unsympathetic. During the process, some of them had also clearly become accustomed to viewing themselves as exceptionally needy or, to use the professional jargon, 'vulnerable', and one has to question whether such a self-image is ultimately helpful to their chances of rehabilitation.

The recent 'Safe in the City' programme piloted an innovative approach to the prevention of youth homelessness, delivering intensive packages of support through multi-agency working ('cluster schemes'). The successful pilot was evaluated through the perceptions of young people who had used it and the key lessons were that support services should be individualised, flexible, focused, accessible, and involving a one-to-one key worker relationship through which all negative influences and barriers could be attacked (Dickens and Woodfield 2004).

In this book we have placed an emphasis on the potentially positive future role of families as providers of ongoing support (see Chapter 6).

Far from ignoring this role, as sometimes happens at the moment, we should be seeking the expansion of work aimed at strengthening family links. These include conciliation and mediation services and various forms of outreach. Services of this type have been comparatively scarce up to the present, because support services for young people have tended to be generic rather than specific, although more specialised services are now expanding rapidly. They have developed in this way because support has been a facet of a service that includes the provision of accommodation, rather than a separate service. Hence a hostel or sup-ported accommodation service may have a team of generic support workers attached to it, who deal with the whole range of housing and support issues. Unfortunately when a young person moves on to another hostel which, as we have seen, is a not infrequent occurrence, the support service also changes. This militates against the development of consistent, supportive relationships that might help young people through a period of instability and crisis.

Furthermore, the variety of problems and issues represented amongst homeless young people is very wide and the case for more spe-cialised forms of support detached from accommodation provision is surely overwhelming. Some of these more specialised support services should concentrate on the role of families. These insights are not unique and, in fact, the development of services for the homeless has been broadly moving in the direction suggested for several years. In Glasgow, for example, a hostel re-provisioning programme is underway (Glasgow Homelessness Partnership 2003) and the principle of the separation of accommodation and support provision has been widely espoused. Understandably, the large antiquated institutions that provide a service mainly for older homeless people have been given priority in this process, in line with the principle of 'worst first'. Many of the hostels for the younger homeless, including those which provided accommodation for many of the young people participating in the Quarriers research, offer relatively high quality facilities and are likely to be amongst the last to be re-provisioned, perhaps many years hence. This is unfortunate because it means that a failing and 'fractured' model of support will be perpetuated.

The ideal model would use hostels and supported accommodation services, located in city centres, only in an emergency and assessment role. The maximum stay in such facilities should be limited to three months, so that kinship and peer networks do not become fractured through the mere passage of time. Thereafter, young people should be housed in tenancies of decent quality, in relation to both the housing itself and its location. One of the main factors utilised in deciding where to offer a tenancy to a young person should be the proximity of friends and family. Support services of various kinds should be delivered to each young person, according to their assessed needs and not on the basis of the location of their accommodation.

An effective pattern of services that will successfully provide young people with a pathway out of homelessness can only be achieved if young people themselves have a major input into the design of those services. In at least one agency providing services for young homeless people in the Glasgow area, formal processes of inclusion have been established to facilitate and encourage the input of young people on service-related issues. It has been recognised that the 'consumer perspective' is essential if services are to be improved with regard to their effectiveness and uptake because the real 'experts' on service provision are the recipients of that service. The evidence of a number of studies suggests the conclusion that homeless young people are more than ready to contribute to their own assessments, if approached in a patient and reassuring manner.

Joint working and effective multi-agency cooperation would undoubtedly prove a feature of the ideal model of service, and the achievement of this would require a significant change in the situation presently prevailing. The recent Shelter survey (Shelter 2005) found that most English authorities do not use multi-agency panels to make homelessness assessments for either 16- to 17-year-olds or 18- to 24-year-olds, although the use of homelessness panels has increased more for the younger age group. In Scotland, local authorities were asked about their use of single shared assessments in relation to homelessness assessments and support package assessments. Although the tool had been increasingly used, still only a minority of authorities employed it for both homelessness assessments and for producing support packages across both age ranges.

Finally, it must be emphasised that the ideal model of future service provision would incorporate ongoing consultation with young people themselves aiming towards their inclusion as stakeholders in the management of the service itself. Despite the many challenges involved in this process, not least the difficulty of engaging young people currently experiencing severe trauma in this kind of activity, it is an essential and not a luxury. Token involvement will not prove useful or adequate. Young people with recent experience of homelessness who are now on the road to a more settled life can be engaged as stakeholders. The Quarriers research demonstrated what is possible in this regard (see Appendix), if their involement in this way can be accomplished, their insights will prove invaluable.

Learning points

- The homelessness service sector appears to lag behind other elements of the UK voluntary sector in various areas, including awareness amongst decision-makers, user involvement and ethnic minority issues.

- Demographic change, housing supply and local authority interpretation of new statutory responsibilities will all have a major impact on the future of youth homelessness.

- An end to priority need status (planned for 2012 in Scotland) is a necessary precursor to the elimination of youth homelessness.

- Local authority interpretations of 'intentionality' will also have an important impact on future numbers of young people presenting as homeless.

- The development of mediation services will be important in strengthening family support but many homeless young people cannot safely return home.

- Rent deposit schemes, supported lodgings schemes, sanctuary schemes and preventative work in schools can all have an impact on reducing homelessness, if sufficiently resourced.

- An effective model of service would accommodate young people away from their home area for only a short assessment period.

- Thereafter, young people should normally be accommodated close to their home area in individual tenancies with a mix of support services closely matched to their needs.

- Effective multi-agency working will be essential to the delivery of this model of service.

- The emphasis placed by young homeless people, themselves, on ordinary values such as homeliness, safety, friendliness, a stimulating environment and the availability of simple support provide a useful guide for the development of future services.

Conclusion

It seems clear that services for young homeless people can be improved and the incidence of homelessness amongst these age groups significantly reduced if the resources were committed and applied effectively. Some ideas have been mooted in this chapter as to how this might be achieved but, of course, this will only happen if a sufficiently powerful political will comes into being. Such a will is not discernable at present and it is quite hard to see how this situation will change while homeless people remain silent and largely invisible. The harsh reality is that few of the nation's voters ever see or hear about a young person who is homeless and, therefore, have little or no awareness of youth homelessness as an issue. Perhaps it is only by giving young homeless people a voice and a platform and the confidence and support to make good use of it that anything will change.

The impetus for this book came from a small-scale research project which is described in the Appendix. The important thing about this project was that it gave young people, innately suspicious of all kinds of professional authority, the security and confidence to speak out for themselves. Even the limited success achieved in this direction was hard-won through a tortuous and difficult process, but it may be the only way to test with any degree of rigor the fitness for purpose of any of the interventions that we are using now or will use in the future. Monies expended on further research of this kind will ultimately save the taxpayer a good deal because it will lead to more effective services. These services, in turn, will provide more direct pathways out of homelessness and away from service-dependence for more of the young people who are currently trapped in the nightmare of homelessness.

References

Bannister, J., Dell, M., Donnison, D., Fitzpatrick, S. and Taylor, R. (1993) *Homeless Young People in Scotland: The Role of the Social Work Services.* Edinburgh: HMSO.

Communities and Local Government (2007) *Statutory Homelessness: First quarter 2007, England.* CLG statistical release 2007/0109 June 2007. London: Department for Communities and Local Government.

Dickens, S. and Woodfield, K. (2004) *New Approaches to Youth Homelessness Prevention: A Qualitative Evaluation of the Safe in the City Cluster Schemes.* York: Joseph Rowntree Foundation.

Fitzpatrick, S. (2000) *Young Homeless People.* Basingstoke: Macmillan.

Glasgow Homelessness Partnership (2003) *Strategy for the Prevention and Alleviation of Homelessness in Glasgow, 2003–2006.* Glasgow: Glasgow Homelessness Partnership.

Jackson, A. (2002) 'Housing for young people: New developments in legislation, ways of working and prevention.' *Housing Care and Support 54,* 4–7.

Saxton, J. and Evans, E. (2002) *The Future of Homelessness? The External Environment and its Impact on Homelessness.* Briefing paper on the future of homelessness as part of the London Housing Foundation's IMPACT programme. London: nfpSynergy.

Shelter (2005) *More Priority Needed: The Impact of Legislative Change on Young Homeless People's Access to Housing and Support.* London: Shelter.

Appendix

The Quarriers Research Project:
How Young People's Views can be Heard

Very little is known about the day-to-day lifestyle of young people who are homeless and who live in the somewhat artificial world of hostels and supported accommodation projects where, to a varying extent, they are forced to share their lives with other young people in a similar situation and staff, charged with the task of helping them to escape from the vicious circle of homelessness. Only very rarely has any attempt been made to study in detail their patterns of activity, their social networks, their family contacts and their sources of help, support and resilience, other than on the basis of anecdote and informal observation. The Quarriers research project aimed to rectify this deficiency.

The overall aim of the research was:

- To learn more about the experience which homeless young people have of the various sources of informal help and support available to them.

This aim was addressed via the following questions:

- What is the nature of the informal support networks with which young homeless people engage on a day-to-day basis and how can these be strengthened?

- What efforts are made to encourage family and peer-group support in ways that can help to promote inclusion and how can they be improved?

- What are the perceptions of young people with regard to the relative merits of different categories of social contact as sources of help and support?

Young homeless people are notoriously difficult to research because of the transitory nature of their lifestyles and their tendency to be preoccupied with serious issues of their own, especially when, as in this instance, the information being sought is 'sensitive'. A number of methodological difficulties presented themselves, particularly in studying peer group relationships and family involvement. For these reasons, a research methodology was devised that involved a very high degree of participation and 'ownership' by young homeless people themselves. From the outset, young people were consulted about the research questions and methodology to gain their perspective on what might be reasonably asked and how answers might be obtained.

Early discussions with young people highlighted an issue that had also been raised at initial meetings with agency representatives – that of drug and alcohol abuse. By the late 1990s professionals within the homelessness field often expressed the view that drugs had become one of the major issues affecting their work. It was undoubtedly true that they were in contact with young people who used drugs on a more regular basis, but it was unclear whether this simply reflected levels of drug use within society generally, or whether there was some truth in the stereotypical view that homelessness and drug abuse were directly linked. This view has often been apparent within the popular press, where the 'homeless junkie' has often assumed the proportions of a 'folk devil'. Young people were asked whether they and their peers would be willing to provide information about issues as personal and sensitive as their social lives, their family relationships and their drug and alcohol use, as well as their personal histories, particularly in relation to their experience of homelessness. The answer, in summary, was that they would, if their trust could be gained, and this depended on the right sort of questions being asked by the right people.

A peer research methodology was devised which involved training a small group of young people, who had experienced homelessness, as researchers. Once trained, they recruited other young homeless people who kept a detailed diary for a two-week period and supported them while they did so. Each diarist was then also interviewed by peer researchers in some depth, using a semistructured schedule, to provide additional contextual information. Once the data gained from the peer research exercise had been subjected to some preliminary analysis, again involving the peer researchers, some tentative conclusions were used to draw up a self-administered questionnaire for homelessness agencies, in order to gain their perspective on the key issues. This innovative mix of methods proved demanding and time-consuming to administer, but was ultimately successful in generating a substantial body of data, providing some unique insights into the real lives of young homeless people.

Every attempt was made to maximise the involvement of the peer researchers and, after the data collection process concluded, with an acceptable number of diaries and interviews completed, ways were sought of involving the young people in the analysis and dissemination of the findings. Several of the peer researchers had expressed enthusiasm for the idea of a residential weekend, during which they could be involved in the first stage of analysis of the accumulated data. Four peer researchers accompanied the two researchers to a small outdoor centre in the Scottish Borders for a residential weekend which combined work with leisure activities. Working in three pairs, the data was divided up, so that each pair could read through their batch of diaries and interviews, discussing and noting themes that were emerging. Then by swapping batches with one of the other pairs, after an agreed interval, everyone had the opportunity to read through all of the data.

In the final session, using the notes taken by the pairs, a general discussion, involving all six present, attempted to reach agreement on an overall list of themes, or preliminary conclusions. Eight such tentative findings were agreed and, once this had been achieved, the findings were never challenged in the group, either during the remainder of the weekend or subsequently. A short narrative report of the weekend was prepared by the researchers and circulated to all the other participants for approval. This report included the eight preliminary findings: the need for user consultation and peer support; the need for support for ongoing family contact; clearer addiction policies; better trained and qualified staff; more constructive activities to fill young people's time; access to computers; help with the high cost of public transport; and faster access to better move-on accommodation.

Although this was intended to be the end of the peer research element of the project, it was agreed that the peer researchers should be given the opportunity to be involved in the dissemination of the preliminary findings, which, it was felt, had their own validity when placed in an appropriate context. Approximately three months after the residential weekend, the group commenced a further series of meetings, during which a PowerPoint presentation was prepared, the text of which was in the peer researchers' own words. A script was also prepared and the presentation delivered on two occasions. The first presentation was to a staff meeting at the residential project for young homeless people, from which the greatest number of peer researchers and research subjects had been recruited. Two months later, the presentation was successfully delivered to a mainly professional audience of around 120, at the Homing-In Conference, the annual conference of the Scottish Youth Housing Network.

The conference marked the formal end of the peer research element of the project, although a great deal of work on data analysis and writing-up continued for the author, for whom it was part of a PhD project. During the peer group phase, a total of 53 young homeless people were involved to varying extents over a 14-month period. During this period a total of 71 meetings, or attempted meetings were arranged, a statistic which illustrates the challenge of organising a project of this kind with this particular client group – young people who, through the effects of homelessness, have lifestyles which are unstable, to a greater or lesser extent.

An overview of the young people participating in the Quarriers research provides a picture of a group of essentially ordinary young people who were very mixed in the range of abilities and characteristics that they possessed. Their only common characteristic was the extraordinary situation in which they were trapped, that of homelessness. In different ways, and to a greater or lesser extent, all had been traumatised by the experience of homelessness. Reaching out to these young people and simply maintaining contact with them, let alone creating a situation of trust where they felt safe enough to tell their stories, proved extremely difficult.

Despite all of these challenges, the research process proved successful in obtaining a body of data and demonstrates that new insights can be obtained by developing these methods further and utilising them on a larger scale. It may be that further research of this type, which gives young homeless people a voice and a platform from which to articulate their own insights, will help to bring about a much-needed reduction in the numbers of those becoming homeless. This will prove especially productive if combined with continued analysis of the reality of their daily lives. If we are to help such young people in the future and reduce this tragic waste of youthful potential, then we must listen to them and understand these experiences in depth. As one of the peer researchers, a young woman aged 21 wrote, after the research finished:

> The research project meant so much to me... People got the chance to tell their stories and that's more important than anything else.

Subject Index

Author Index